The Zen of Love

The Zen of Love

DISCOVER YOUR OWN AWAKENED HEART

Peter Cutler

N-lightenment LLC
SEDONA, AZ

Copyright © 2017 by Peter Cutler.

All rights reserved. No part of this publication may be reproduced, distributed or transmitted in any form or by any means, including photocopying, recording, or other electronic or mechanical methods, without the prior written permission of the publisher, except in the case of brief quotations embodied in critical reviews and certain other noncommercial uses permitted by copyright law. For permission requests, contact the author through his website n-lightenment.com or email at peter@n-lightenment.com.

Website: http://n-lightenment.com

Email: peter@n-lightenment.com

N-lightenment LLC
120 Birch Blvd.
Sedona, AZ 86336

Cover art Zen Brush painting by Peter Cutler. More paintings can be seen on the gallery section of the website.

Ordering Information:

This book is available in print, e-book and audio. You can find it on Amazon.com or contact the author / publisher directly.

The Zen of Love/ Peter Cutler. —1st edition.

ISBN: 978-1540794796

What Readers Say:

"Peter Cutler is a Buddha, a regular man who has somehow awakened. Just read his words and it is evident. His words are carried with light. He is a Mystic for our time. I am deeply grateful."
 – Lin Shanti Goodman

The Zen of Love is one of the clearest books ever written on the fundamentals of spirituality and personal growth. In its pages the philosophy of Zen meets the most practical aspects of love and relationship (with self and others). Author, Peter Cutler, combines deep insights, warm anecdotes, and effective exercises to awaken the reader's heart and mind through authentic love and compassion."
 – Michael Mirdad, Spiritual Teacher *Creating Fulfilling Relationships* and *Healing the Heart & Soul*

"*The Zen of Love* is an absolutely wonderful book – highly compelling and beautifully written. Its openhearted message of love positively beams from every page."
 – Rosina Wilson

"*The Zen of Love* is worthy of high praise. The book immediately elicits a palpable and tangible experience of the love which it speaks. I began reading it and by page three melted into the ineffable essence of the author's writing. If you are seeking a book about spiritual awakening / enlightenment which contains more than just words, you've just found it."
 – J. Stewart Dixon *Blue Collar Enlightenment*

"A lot of Truth spoken here."
 – Edythe Currie

"More than just a book, it is a timeless path to share with all who can touch the wisdom and peace conveyed in every chapter."
 – Mary Lou Christianson

"In *The Zen of Love*, Peter speaks to the reader intimately and personally in a way that is compelling, and, through his words, conveys the love that he so eloquently speaks about. It is no surprise that Peter would write about love when he so naturally and deeply embodies it."
 – Gina Lake, *Choosing Love, The Heroic Journey* and *Radical Happiness*

"This writing comes from the Heart and speaks directly to the Heart. While reading these passages, I felt the gentle stirrings of recognition within."
 – Carolyn Marsden

"It is so good to read this! I can already feel this love while only reading. And now I do this practice! Thank you, Peter."
 – Stina Brunner

"Thank you. This is inspired and brilliant. Thank you!"
 – Stephen Benny Benedict

"Was walking around all today thinking of LOVE, Peter. I "blame" you. Gratefully."
 – Nic Holmes

"Many thanks, Peter, for sharing so much clear, insightful and profound wisdom with us all. Your words resonate with the inner essence of all. Infinite love and gratitude."
 – Barbara Carter

Contents

Acknowledgments xiii
Forward xv
1. Introduction 1
2. Did You Choose This Book? *Or Did This Book Choose You?* 5
3. The Heart Is Very Happy 9
4. I Love You 11
5. How to Have the Most Perfect Relationship on Earth 15
6. My First Girlfriend 25
7. Falling in Love with Love 29
8. My Amazing Revelation at Sixteen 33
9. Love Cannot Cause Pain 35
10. A Message of Love 39
11. Falling in Love with Truth 43
12. Being Awake 49
13. The Story of My Awakening 53
14. The Heart Song 63
15. An Exercise in Love and Awakening 67
16. All There Is Is Love 73

17. Falling in Love with Love Part Two 77
18. The Eyes of Love 81
19. To Know Thyself Is to Love Thyself 83
20. The Glorious Impossibility of Loving Yourself 87
21. The Game...91
22. The Dream..95
23. We Are All Dreamers 99
24. You Can Dream Anything You Want 103
25. The Mystic's Guide to Dating 105
26. Real Love Is Unconditional....................................117
27. Sex and the Spiritual Path 119
28. Invaluable Lessons of Heartbreak 125
29. Two Relationships – How and Why We Choose Suffering over Love 131
30. The Doorway Home 135
31. The Dance of Leela..137
32. The Purpose of Every Relationship......................141
33. For Ahna 147
34. Relationships and Love 149
35. The World of True Love 153
36. You Are Already Happy. You Were Just Too Busy Arguing to Notice. 161
37. Love Is the Only Real Medicine 167
38. The Song Of Love 171

39. A Special Gift	175
40. Love and Fear	179
41. A Love Letter	181
42. Death Does Not End True Love	185
43. The Rose And You	189
44. Exercise – Feeling Love Everywhere	193
45. What Is Awakening? What Is Enlightenment?	197
46. Expand the Circle	201
47. The Circle	205
48. You ARE Love	209
49. Unconditional Love	211
50. The Silent Saint	213
51. It Is All for Your Benefit	217
52. I Am Only Writing to My Self	219
53. I Love You	221
Resources	227
About the Author	229

Acknowledgments

WITH GREAT LOVE AND GRATITUDE I thank my many teachers, without whom this book would not have been possible. It is a long list, so, Dear Reader, you do not have to read it through. My heart is overflowing with gratitude and so compels it. My spiritual teachers are many, as really all of life is constantly teaching me. But I will single out these names as perhaps the most important.

Thich Nhat Hanh, Mooji, Eckhart Tolle, Zen Master Seung Sahn, Douglas Harding (Headless Way), Steve Brown, Shunru Suzuki, Dogen, Sahajananda, Adyashanti, Papaji, Ramana Maharshi, Peace Pilgrim, Buddha, Jesus, Lao Tzu, *Heart Sutra*, *A Course in Miracles*, Byron Katie, Gina Lake, Nirmala, Alok Hsu Kwan-han, Joanne Friday, John Bell, David Hoffmeister, Bill Spain, Sarah Joy Naegle (the Silent Saint you will read about later in this book).

My family members who, whether they knew it or not, have all been my spiritual teachers: Judith Cutler, Lindsay Cutler, Rachel Cutler Costello, Grace Cutler, Noah Cutler, Jamie Chapman, my sister Starr and brother Dave, my mother Anne, my father Jack, my stepmother Marrietta, my aunts Patricia Warner, Judith Shinkle and Susan Alderich, whose love, along with the love of my maternal grandfather William Hoffman and my paternal grandmother Rosalind Cutler, went a long way towards keeping my heart alive; and my uncle Peter who I was named after, an innocent, good-natured blessing on this world if there ever was one, much like my brother Dave. Both have physically passed on, but have never for a single moment left my heart.

To my dear friends and loved ones who have such a deep place in my heart.

To Tom Bird, Rama, Gwen and Rosina Wilson for helping

this book come to life in such an effortless, loving and joyful flow. To Gina Lake for being such an invaluable guide.

And my students who are too many to name, but be assured you are always as much my teacher as I am yours. This book is really dedicated to you and all the students to come. Without your questions and deep longing to awaken, I would have nothing to teach or write. This book could not have happened without you. Thank you, my beloved students. This is your book far more than it is mine.

Forward

There is a traditional Sufi saying that in all of creation there are only two: Lover and Beloved. It is possible to realize (similar to Christ's mystical knowing, "I and the Father are One") that I and the Lover/Beloved are One/Self. With this knowing comes a sense of unity with "all that is," for everyone is both Lover and Beloved, and separation is an illusion. Metaphorically speaking, Peter Cutler has been to these heights of realization; and like the freed prisoner in Plato's Allegory of the Cave, he has returned to tell of Reality beyond the shadows of illusion.

The Zen of Love: Discover Your Own Awakened Heart is a spiritual guidebook explaining the inexplicable—how the unified vision of Self-realization (Spirit) interfaces with the world of separation and duality, or how the One of Unity and the many of separation merge through the power and presence of Love. In down-to-earth, tell-it-like-it-is language, examples, and exercises, the author makes simple this seemingly impossible and complex task of using the language of duality to reveal the transcendent unifying power of Love.

The beauty of this book is that its content is understandable, meaningful, and inspiring to any reader, whether advanced or beginning on the spiritual path, or journey Home. Written from the heart of the author to the heart of the reader, the message of this book reduces enlightenment to the bare essential—the realization of Love as Oneself that includes everyone.

Chosen at random from *The Zen of Love*, the following quotes bear witness to the beauty and wisdom of the content of this inspiring book:

". . . the only real Truth there is is Love. . . . We experience difficulties because we forget this Truth and act out of imagined separation . . . and all the incredible pain and suffering that comes from this simple forgetting can also be used to point us

Home again."

"Love means the end of separation. That is all it means. And this feels very good. There is nothing that a separate human can experience that even comes close to this."

"Ultimate Truth and unconditional Love . . . are both not separate from what you are."

"You are an expression of the Divine Self dancing with Itself. . . Love is really simply the Self seeing and recognizing the Self. . . If you look with awakened eyes you too can see this. You are at once the Self that is looking and the Supreme Self that is being seen. Everywhere you are only seeing your Self."

And last, but not least, the following chapter title says it all, capturing the insanity of the split mind: "You Are Already Happy—You Were Just Too Busy Arguing to Notice."

– Rev. Lynne R. Matous, M.A., Interfaith minister and editor

CHAPTER ONE

Introduction

THIS BOOK IS A JOURNEY not of the outer world, but of an inner world even more amazing and rewarding than you can now imagine. It is here, just waiting for you to open the door or turn the page. Think of this book as your loving guide to the unexplored world of you.

It is not the only book that can guide you on this very special inner journey. There have been many others: *A Course in Miracles*, Eckhart Tolle's *The Power of Now*, Thich Nhat Hanh's *The Miracle of Mindfulness*, Advaita Master Mooji's *White Fire*, to name just a few recent ones. I highly recommend each one and the others you'll find in the Resources section of my website. But there is a very special reason you picked up this particular book at this particular time.

This is a book about love. It will improve your relationships – miraculously so if you honestly follow its suggestions. If you're not in a relationship, it will teach you the secret of irresistible magnetic attraction. And even more importantly, this book will transform your relationship with yourself. Few people actually love themselves, and this is at the center of all relationship problems. This book will show you, once and for all, how to truly love yourself.

There is enormous value in improving, repairing, and even saving relationships, finding a fulfilling relationship, and learning how to truly love yourself. But that's just the start. And this is where this book about love is radically different from most. If you're willing and ready to take this journey to the end of the ride, if you're willing to follow the call of love to its natural and inevitable conclusion, this book will open your eyes, heart and mind to the Truth of life as it really is. This book will awaken you.

I understand that's a lot to take in. How can a book do what possibly years of spiritual practices, traditions and teachers have not? My answer is that these are new times, this is a new book, and this is a new you. Give it a try and see for yourself. Read it with an open mind and open heart and I believe you will find what your heart is seeking.

I've been a spiritual seeker for much of my life. Although my childhood was challenging, even before I was ten years old, when I was alone I often experienced being filled with a powerful light and love I did not understand. I called it the "presence of God." I began the study of yoga and meditation when I was only sixteen. At the age of twenty-two, I experienced a profound awakening, which I describe in detail in this book. After only ten days of this extraordinary bliss I fell back into the common dream state most of us consider our life. The brief taste of this profound state of consciousness, and its rapid ending, brought a new urgency to my spiritual search in the following years.

I became a student of the Vietnamese Buddhist monk Thich Nhat Hanh and was ordained into his Order of Interbeing with the Dharma name True Sangha Virtue. I also studied with Korean Zen Master Seung Sahn, meditation teacher Jack Kornfield, Mindfulness teacher Jon Kabbot-Zinn, Advaita Master Mooji, *A Course in Miracles* teachers David Hoffmeister and Marianne Williamson, and many others. I read every spiritual book I could get my hands on and became a teacher of meditation.

And all this time I lived an ordinary life with the comings and goings of intimate relationships, two marriages, raising a family of four children, overcoming cancer, and creating and building a very demanding and successful career as a commercial artist, photographer and film director. I met the love of my life many times, but something always got in the way. At the time I didn't realize it was me. I achieved the height of success in my career, receiving over one hundred international awards from film festivals, only to find that all of this didn't bring me the elusive happiness I sought. I didn't know who I truly was, so how could anything truly fulfill me?

As I began to awaken again, my life dramatically changed. In 2010, I moved from Boston, Massachusetts to Sedona, Arizona, founded and ran a spiritual retreat center called the Sacred Circle, and became a spiritual teacher and healer. But what was happening on the inside was far more important and amazing. No longer did I seek fulfillment outside. I realized I was already one hundred percent complete – and always had been. The happiness and peace I sought outside was already in here, and it was in here no matter what was happening around me. The love I had always sought outside had never been separate from me, nor had anything or anyone else. It became crystal clear that my self, my life and the world were nothing like I had always believed them to be. And this was such a relief. Struggle was over. Freedom was here. I just hadn't realized it before. I had been living in a dream. But I still had something very important to learn. Actually learning never ends, but this particular learning relates very much to this book, and to you.

During a seven-month silent retreat in 2014, much to my surprise, I realized that my awakening had not come only from those deep spiritual practices, but even more so from the very ordinary experiences of my day-to-day life that I had once perceived as obstacles. Even more specifically, my awakening had come from love. And that was the birth of this book. My awakening had come from each beautiful, soul-stirring moment of love, and even more from each messy, painful, and even traumatic moment. This is wonderful news for you. Each moment from the very day I was born, life had been teaching me to wake up. And this is just as true for you. For quite some time I didn't pay attention. And then – suddenly – I did.

If I told you that to awaken you must climb to the top of a Himalayan mountain and find a certain wise man living in a cave, or leave your family and spend the next ten years in a monastery, or even do many of the more extreme spiritual practices I have done, would that really be practical? The good news is that I'm telling you that right now – in the very middle of your messy day-to-day life, with all the challenging relationships, demands and obligations – that these very things are not obstacles to happiness and spiritual awakening, but instead are the very key to it. This is what I discovered. This is how this book was born. And this is what this book will help you discover for yourself.

If you read this book with an open heart and open mind, it will bring vibrant new life to your relationships. It will connect you to your heart's true desire. It will fill your heart with a love you never believed was possible. And this book will awaken you to the miracle of life as it truly is.

May this book be the next page in your exciting new life.

Let's turn the page now and begin.
With all my love,
Peter

CHAPTER TWO

Did You Choose This Book?
Or Did This Book Choose You?

IT MAY BE NO EXAGGERATION TO SAY that this book can transform your life. It will certainly transform your relationships with other people, with God (or whatever word you choose for something greater than yourself) and, most importantly, it will transform the relationship you have with yourself.

This is a special book. Perhaps you've never read another book quite like it. It is a book written specifically for you. And before you're done reading it, perhaps you will realize the part you played in its creation.

A little over a year ago I entered a seven-month silent retreat. I called this "descending into the Cave of the Heart." As a spiritual teacher and healer, I had done this many times before. But this was different.

It became clear to me that my teaching needed to go even deeper. As an awakened spiritual teacher, you experience life in a very different way from most people. You no longer identify as a separate, isolated person, so you no longer suffer. You realize the inherent perfection in all that is. People experience your peace, love and joy when they are in your presence. It triggers their own natural state of being. And this is very beautiful and helpful. But still there was something missing.

The missing element was a bridge between the awakened

consciousness of the teacher and the consciousness of the student who was still experiencing a life of separation, incompleteness and suffering. Although I didn't realize it when I began this period of deep silence and reflection, it was this bridge that was waiting for me. It was this bridge that was calling me.

For years I'd been teaching what I had been taught to help people awaken. And these were wonderful teachings, traditions and practices. I am eternally grateful for them and for my teachers.

While I was teaching, there was often this gap between what I was experiencing and what my students experienced. Try as I might, this gap remained. My students learned many things and grew a great deal, but still this gap remained. All spiritual teachers experience this gap. I needed a bridge to connect my students to what I experience, a bridge of consciousness. Spiritual teachings are of limited value if they are understood with the mind alone. They must be experienced on a very deep level that transforms everything in a person's life.

During the fifth month of the retreat, this bridge was revealed to me. I learned much from my teachers and the different traditions and practices that had become such a big part of my life. But the truth was that I had awakened through love. And not only spiritual love, but the messy love of day-to-day relationships. From the moment of my birth on Valentine's Day, I had been learning to awaken through love. I realized this was the bridge that could help others awaken too. In every experience of love, there is a powerful seed of pure, enlightened being. And this is what the book will reveal to you, just as it did for me. I also realized that this is not my book, but yours. It was written for you.

But it was not written for your mind, as so many books are. No one figures out how to be enlightened. It is a direct experience. And only this direct experience can help you.

This book is speaking to a much deeper place than your

mind. It is speaking to your heart. To get the most from the book, please don't rush through it. There are sections that need your deepest attention. You may want to stop frequently and experience what is happening inside you. Pay close attention to these feelings. The book will work on you in ways you do not yet understand. Please trust this process. It is here for you. And you will be very grateful for it.

You might say the book will work on you from the inside out. Everything in this book is already in you. You just may not be aware of it yet. But you will be.

The book will bring you to a deep and powerful experience of love you have likely never tasted before. And when you do, it will literally transform your life. Think of this book as a friend who is guiding you to a place you have longed for, but never believed you could find. It can do that for you if you truly listen, not only to the book, but to what is happening within you as you read it.

You might even say a part of you has written this book to yourself. Deep inside your heart, you already know everything you will read here. But for quite some time now, you have not listened. Your thoughts have obscured the infinite intelligence of your heart. This book will remind you. It will help you listen again. And you will be very happy.

On New Year's Eve a friend mentioned that his goal for the New Year was to communicate more through silence than through words. This is a very high-level aspiration. It filled me with joy, love and gratitude just to hear it. We have become so skilled at using words, and thinking in words, that we have forgotten our ability to communicate on a deeper level than words can touch. And, although this book contains many words, it too is communicating on a deeper level than words can touch. As you read this book, as you embark on this sacred journey of the heart, please take a moment to listen to what is being spoken in the silent spaces between the words. Take a moment to listen to the silent space deep in your own heart, which even now may be responding to this very special form of communication. The Sufis call this the Sacred Tremor of the Heart. And, if you listen very carefully, I know you will hear it. For this is truly the Path of the Awakened Heart. And it begins with you. It has always begun with you. And right now it is beginning again.

CHAPTER THREE

The Heart Is Very Happy

EVERYTHING WRITTEN IN THESE PAGES
is already written in your heart.

That is why you respond as you do.
That is how you know it is true.

Before you ever read it,
you knew it.

You have always known it.

The words in these pages are just a reminder.

I have nothing new to tell you.
I have nothing new to say.
Don't read with your mind that compares and contrasts.
Read with your heart and you will see that this is true.

Everything I write your heart already knows.
Your heart has always known.
Read with your heart.
Listen with your heart.
And you will know this is True.

The Zen of Love

The world has many new things to offer you.
It is always offering something new and interesting.
It offers the promise of great things to come.
It offers wonderful and exciting food for the mind.

But I offer nothing new.
I only offer what your heart already knows.
I only offer what your heart already has.

The mind has no use for what I offer.
It speaks a very different language.

But the heart, oh the heart,
it has found a kindred spirit.
It has found one of its own.
And it is very happy.

CHAPTER FOUR

I Love You

I LOVE YOU, my Dear Beloved Reader. This may seem an odd way to begin a book. But it is true. And ever since my Awakening, I can only speak the truth. You could say this is a love letter directly to you, My Beloved.

When I say I love you, you must know the love I speak of. This love has no conditions. It is incapable of discriminating or judging. It knows no gender, no age, no race. It sees neither beauty nor ugliness, but only your absolute holy perfection. It does not care what you have done or what you will do, but only what you are. And you are this same perfect love I feel right now as I write this love letter to you, My Beloved. This love I speak of is very simple. It knows only love. And it knows love completely.

Simple as it is, this love is the most powerful force in the universe. It heals the sick and brings the spiritually dead back to life. Unlike everything we perceive in this world, love is unchanging, limitless, infinite and eternal.

And this is the love I feel for you. By my loving you in this way, you are free to feel this unconditional love for yourself. And this is how the world is healed.

You may wonder how I can love you when I don't even know you. And that would be true – except that I do know you. I know you intimately. I know you as well as I know my own self. I know every secret, fear, doubt and judgment you are now holding in your heart. And still I love you utterly, completely and unconditionally. You see, you and I are not unalike. We are not strangers: far from it.

If you look deep into your heart you will find that we share the same heart, My Beloved. We are One. I know you may find this hard to believe now. But before you finish this book, you will discover it is true. There is only One Heart. It is not yours personally. Nor is it mine. It is one shared Heart. One Love. And it sings One Heart Song.

It is so glorious. It is singing right now in these pages. It is traveling to you through these words. This book is much more than paper and ink. It is more than words, sentences and paragraphs. You might say this book itself is love. Right now you are holding love in your hands. Each word is love. The paper and ink are infused with love. Each word carries the magical perfume of love. Read deeply. Let the words wash over you, removing all doubts and fears, revealing the infinite and eternal love that is right now humming in your breast and bringing life to every cell.

This love is the most powerful force in the universe. It is infinite. It is eternal. And it is right here in this book, singing in the spaces between each word, each sentence, each paragraph. Can you hear it? It is your Heart Song. And that is why right now it is speaking to you. It is traveling to you through these very words.

You might, for just a moment, stop reading now and simply hold this book up to your heart. Close your eyes. Now listen. Can you hear your Heart Song? It is the same as mine. This is a Song we all share. There is only one Heart Song. Listen. Feel it reverberate in your Heart. Please know that it has always been here. It was here in your mother's womb, and even before that. This Song we share is older than time itself. It is more vast than space. Listen. Can you hear it?

It may now sound like only the faintest whisper. But trust me, My Love, it is louder than all sounds combined. For in every molecule that has ever existed, this same Heart Song is singing.

Discover Your Own Awakened Heart

Listen. I know you can hear it if you truly listen.

You may experience it as an expanding in your chest, a tingling, an excitement in your body's cells. You might even hear a sound, but more likely it will be a feeling. And this feeling is universal. There is no human who has not felt this Song of the Heart.

And this Heart Song, this love, is Enlightenment. It is God. For so long, humans have searched for Enlightenment. For so long we have longed to experience God. And here all along, singing in our very own Heart, was everything we have ever searched for.

For you see, Beloved, it is the very same love that you have felt. The same love that you have touched that is not only the path to God, to Enlightenment, but God Itself. It is the map, the journey and the completion of the journey. It is the beginning, the middle and the end all rolled into one. And never, not for one blessed instant, have you ever been apart from it.

Amazing, isn't it? What you have searched for in vain, lifetime after lifetime, was always as close as that familiar tug on your heartstrings when you gazed into the eyes of a baby, cried during a romantic movie, or sank into the deep kiss of your Beloved for the very first time. Yes, right here all this time was God. You have never for a moment not been Enlightened. You just didn't know. You were not aware. You forgot. You thought love was something else. Yes, it felt good. Sometimes you chased it, craved it, longed for it. But you never really understood the profound nature of what love really is. You thought it was something precious, limited, in short supply. You thought only the very lucky or beautiful experienced it. But this cannot be so, Beloved. For right now already your heart is beginning to sing, beginning to remember. What you are remembering is who you are. For you yourself are love. And not just the limited thing you had thought was love. You are Real Love. You are Divine Love, infinite and eternal. Nothing can harm or lessen this love even a micro-millimeter. It is permanent and unchanging.

The Zen of Love

It may be surprising to learn, with all these stories of divorce and perhaps your own experience, but love never changes. It is impossible to lose it. It is impossible to have less or more love. It is impossible for it to fade. You only believe or experience this because you don't yet understand what love is or what you are. As I have said, love is infinite and eternal. And this bears repeating until you understand. There is no place that love is not. And some say, and this is what I experience: only love is real. In all of this incredible world filled with seeming variety – war and peace, wealth and poverty, good and bad, beauty and ugliness – all that actually exists is love. And that is the reason why I say that I love you. For nothing else that I say can be true. I call you my Dearest Love because you are that to me. Even now I see you as you read these lines. And not only that: I feel you right here in my own Heart, this Heart that holds the entire world within it, this same Heart that has never known anything but love. And so when I say that I love you, this is the truest thing I can ever say. And perhaps someday or even right now, this very moment, you can say this too. You can feel this One Heart beating in your own chest. You can feel it resonating in this enormous, infinite field of love. Can you feel it right now?

If not now, do not worry. It will come. It must, because trust me, My Dearest One, it is right here. Even now, in the midst of your suffering, your sorrow, your dark night, this flame of love is burning brightly. If you can sense just a spark of it, just one glowing ember, do not worry. Let this spark grow. Let this ember glow brighter. Let a small blaze begin. And let this blaze grow and continue growing until you feel a mighty fire of love. And let this Heart Fire burn away all the sorrow, suffering and pain of this imagined life. For I tell you that no matter what you have experienced so far in your life, only love is real. Let me say that again. Only Love Is Real.

CHAPTER FIVE

How to Have the Most Perfect Relationship on Earth

THERE HAVE BEEN MANY GREAT RELATIONSHIPS in the history of humankind, both literary and real. Anthony and Cleopatra. Romeo and Juliet. Rhett and Scarlett. Harry and Sally. But none were lasting. All were short lived. And, steamy as they may have been, none of them could be called perfect. Romeo and Juliet's affair ended in suicide. And there were certainly challenges in all of them. Even Cinderella and the Prince's story ends with their marriage. We don't really know what happens next. Does happily ever after mean the marriage our parents had?

This appears to be humankind's best hope for a relationship. This is as good as it gets. At best it has its ups and downs. What we hope for are more ups than downs. What we usually get is a mix. And this is what we settle for. We don't know there is a far happier, more loving and more perfect relationship available to all of us. And this is what I'm going to share with you.

The Mirror Exercise

To start with, I'm going to ask you to do a simple exercise that will reveal important insights into all your current and past relationships. It is very simple. What I want you to do is look into a mirror. Look straight into your eyes. And simply say, to your reflection, "I love you." If you are a little braver, do this nude in a full-length mirror. It works better this way. Just keep repeating this one simple sentence over and over again: "I love you." Keep saying to yourself, "I love you." Do this for five minutes. Use a timer because it's important that you maintain eye contact with your reflection in the mirror the entire time.

What I experience when I do this is increasing and deepening waves of love. What you experience will likely be something quite different. You will experience what I experienced when I first started doing this exercise years ago. You will experience your relationship with yourself. And it's a mixed relationship. It has ups and downs, just like your relationships with others.

As you continue saying the words "I love you" to yourself, you will sometimes feel a wonderful, warm love embracing you – but at other times you'll feel something very different and not nearly so pleasant. You will feel things like "I'm not good enough." "If people knew me they wouldn't love me." "I'm a fraud." "If only I were thinner." "If only my breasts were larger." "If only my breasts were smaller." "If only I were taller." "If only I were smarter." "If only I were more beautiful." "If only I were more handsome." "Just look at those wrinkles." "I'm losing my hair." "How could anyone love someone who did what I did?" "I don't deserve love." All these thoughts and more will begin bubbling up from your unconscious. While you're verbally expressing love to yourself, these deeply hidden and sometimes not so hidden thoughts tell a very different story. They express what you're really thinking about yourself.

When these thoughts start bubbling up and contradicting the love you're verbally expressing, many people stop the exercise right there. These thoughts feel so yucky they don't want to continue. But I'm asking you to continue anyway. Just keep saying "I love you" to yourself. Let the yucky thoughts come up. They're your thoughts. It's wonderful they're being exposed now. These thoughts are the source of the problems you're having, not only in your relationship with yourself, but also in every single relationship you have now and ever have had with others.

The relationship you have with yourself is projected out onto every relationship you have. Your relationship with others is a mirror of the relationship you have with yourself. What you don't love about yourself is going to reflect on what you won't love about others. The way to heal your relationship with others is to heal your relationship with yourself.

This is not what we're taught in our society. And because of this, relationships have a lot of problems. In the US, fifty percent of marriages end in divorce. These are not perfect relationships. But they can be. And I will show you how.

It Starts with You

When you notice those yucky thoughts that arise in this exercise, pay close attention to them and how they make you feel – but also, don't take them so seriously. None of them are true. And yet they do clearly affect you. Notice how these unpleasant feelings also come up at other times in your life. If you drop a glass and it shatters on the floor, is there an inner voice of condemnation that immediately shouts, "Clumsy!" or "Idiot"? And possibly it continues with other thoughts that are anything but loving. "Why did I do that?" "I should know better." "I should be more careful."

This relationship you're having with your thoughts is not only happening during this exercise. It's happening throughout your life. You're probably not aware how often you criticize and condemn yourself. Pay attention to your thoughts throughout even one day and you'll be surprised. This is the relationship you have with yourself. Is it a good one? Is it based on love, respect, gratitude and joy? Or is it based on criticism, condemnation, judgment and abuse? Those critical voices have many sources: parents, siblings, teachers, friends, lovers, coaches, employers. Anyone who has ever criticized or judged you can be the source of your inner critic.

Because your inner state actually creates your external world, this critical inner voice is also how you experience those around you. These judgmental thoughts create your relationships, and all the problems you experience in them. This accounts for the fifty-percent divorce rate and all the problems you face in your own relationship, both now and in the past. This is exactly why you're not now experiencing a perfect relationship. But there is good news.

Change Your Thoughts and the World Changes

To have a good relationship with others, you must first have a good relationship with yourself. You've heard it said before: to love others, you first need to love yourself. And this is absolutely true. Those critical thoughts in your head are not loving thoughts. They're abusive. As long as you believe those thoughts, you're having an abusive relationship with yourself. This is not a loving relationship. Until you have a loving relationship with yourself, you can't really have one with anyone else. But here's the good news.

You Can Love Yourself

Continue the exercise with the mirror. Recognize that those critical thoughts that keep arising are merely thoughts and nothing more. They are simply conditions you place on your love. "If only I wasn't so fat I could love myself." "If only I weren't bald, I could love myself." We have so many "if onlys." If one "if only" is satisfied, another one will instantly take its place. It seems we will never be good enough to deserve our own love. This is called conditional love. And conditional love will always have some condition that is not satisfied. Our thoughts are nothing more than a series of conditions we place on ourselves to prevent us from loving ourselves. And it's very effective, isn't it?

Loving ourselves conditionally will never work. We can never be thin enough, rich enough, successful enough, famous enough or beautiful enough to satisfy this critical inner voice. We need to learn to love ourselves without any conditions at all. And this is much easier than you think.

Unconditional Love

Unconditional love simply means love without any conditions. We look at ourselves in the mirror. We see wrinkles and still we love. We see fat and still we love. No matter what we see, we love. What we really see is not so much a limited person with all its flaws and limitations, but love itself. When we look at our reflection in the mirror we just see love. This is what I see when I do this exercise. Yes, I see wrinkles, baldness, all the same things you see when you look at a limited human body. But what I really see is love itself. All those limitations fade into the background of something so much greater.

Something Much Greater

I use the word God and sometimes Zen and sometimes Tao. To me these words are interchangeable, as are all words that point to something that cannot truthfully be described or even imagined with the human mind. Someone else may use the word Rama, Shiva, Krishna, Brahma, Allah, Yahweh or Great Spirit. Some spiritual teachers use the word Universal Consciousness or Awareness. There are many names, but no name can describe this experience. An atheist may experience this something greater when he looks at the stars filling a night sky or the Grand Canyon or a mountain range at sunset. He may call this something greater Nature or the Universe. We have all at one time or another experienced something greater than the limited being we call I. And when we experience this something greater, we somehow feel that we are also greater than we felt just a moment ago. Where before we felt alone and separate, in that moment we feel connected. That experience is what I call God. You can call it Nature, Rama, Consciousness or whatever you like. I don't mind at all. Neither does God.

The reason I bring up God at this time is because God is unconditional love. God is the experience of unconditional love. As you've experienced, our human mind has many thoughts, judgments and conditions about us, and whether we deserve love, and under what conditions we deserve love. God has no such conditions. God simply loves. No matter what you look like, what is happening in your life or even if you are being your most self-critical, God can do nothing but love you. And the truth is that this unconditional love is the love you deserve, and always have deserved. You just didn't know it yet. And here it is. It has never gone anywhere. You have always been loved absolutely unconditionally. Not just by God, but by you. If you let those critical, judging, conditional thoughts fade away for just a moment, all you experience is love. This is what I experience. And you can experience this too. Why not? It is always here. It's never gone anywhere.

It might be easier if you first learn to see yourself through God's eyes. That's why I bring up God. Right now you still believe you are a limited person filled with limitations, guilt and flaws. But you know that God, Rama, Consciousness, Spirit, Nature or the Universe are not like that. They are something more. They are something much more. And until you realize you are too, let this concept help you.

You Are Much More Than You Think

Try another exercise for a moment. This is something I teach in Tai Chi classes. You will need two people for this exercise.

1. Stand with your feet a little more than hip width

apart. Your friend is going to push you from the side. I want you to resist his or her push with all your might. Lean into your friend to prevent him or her from pushing you over. Use all your strength and power to prevent yourself from being moved.

2. Now take a different approach. Keep your feet in exactly the same position. I want you to imagine your hips, legs and feet are the trunk of a great tree. The roots of this tree extend from your feet all the way to the center of the earth. These roots wrap around the core of the earth. If you pay attention, you can even feel the energy of the core of the earth moving up and feeding your roots and trunk. I want you to think of your body above your hips as the upper trunk of the tree. While the bottom trunk is firmly rooted to the earth, the upper trunk is more flexible so it can move with the wind. Just settle into this. Relax. There is no need to tense your muscles or resist the push. When you're ready, ask your friend to push you again.

What you discover is that when your body is tense and you resist with all your might, it is easy for your friend to push you over. When you take the second approach, even though you're not resisting, you cannot be moved. You have become as much as ten times more powerful, simply by thinking different thoughts.

So who are you? When you resist being pushed with all your might, you are limited, weak, and relatively powerless, like a piece of straw blowing in the wind. But when you connect with the earth, even just with your imagination, you suddenly have ten times the power without any effort at all. A more extreme example of this is a tiny, hundred-pound Tai Chi master who cannot be moved an inch by six burly football players.

Take turns doing this exercise with your friend so you can

experience the immovable power you have, simply through changing your thoughts.

Thoughts Are Powerful

Your thoughts are powerful, as long as you believe them. But you don't have to believe them. When you stop paying attention to your thoughts even for a moment, you experience a profound freedom you never knew existed.

Ten-Second Enlightenment Exercise

It may be quite difficult to stop paying attention to your thoughts for a full day, but how about for only ten seconds? For just ten seconds, don't pay any attention to your thoughts. Allow them to arise as they will, but don't give them any attention. Instead, notice life without thoughts. Notice your breath moving in and out. Notice sounds. Notice how your body feels. Notice that your body is filled with energy in every part of it. Notice that you are alive. Without thoughts interfering, you'll notice things in life you've never experienced before. It's wonderful, isn't it? The more we experience being free from thoughts, the more freedom we have from those critical thoughts that prevent us from loving ourselves unconditionally. They are just thoughts. They don't need your belief or attention.

Back to the Mirror

Let's go back to our mirror exercise with these new tools we've learned. Continue with the "I love you" exercise. Now, when negative or critical thoughts arise, simply allow them to come up, stay for a moment and move on. They're not important. Let them move through your mind like clouds gliding across an infinite blue sky.

The clouds do not affect the sky. And your thoughts don't affect you unless you allow them to. Let thoughts come and go.

Continue looking into your eyes. When thoughts stop interfering, you can begin to see something else in the mirror, something you didn't see before. You begin to see what is behind the eyes. You begin to see love. You begin to see, not the usual self of thoughts, but a Self that has always been here but hidden behind all those thoughts. And this Self you cannot help but love. It is love itself. Now you are truly seeing with the Eyes of God or the Eyes of Zen or the Eyes of Tao or whatever you choose to call it. You are seeing your True Self through the eyes of your True Self. And this is the perfect relationship. This is unconditional love. When you experience this, you will see all your relationships through these same eyes. You will see this same unconditional love in everyone you set eyes on. This is the love that lies hidden behind thoughts, bodies and appearances. This is the perfect relationship.

And when we truly love ourselves in this unconditional way, all our other relationships take on this same quality. With or without a partner, you will always have this perfect relationship. You will have the most perfect relationship on Earth.

CHAPTER SIX

My First Girlfriend

I WAS FOUR OR FIVE YEARS OLD when I met my neighbor Ginny. We instantly became best friends, as children that age often do. She was one year younger than me and adored me. And I adored her too. We would spend our afternoons lying in the tall grass of a nearby field, so our parents couldn't see us, planning our escape. We had decided we could live for the rest of our lives in this tall grass. It would become our home. When we were old enough we would get married. That was our plan anyway. At the end of the day, after much parental yelling and searching, we always ended up reluctantly returning home.

Ginny was my first girlfriend and also my first friend. We were only young children but we loved each other. There can be no doubt of that. We were inseparable.

At age six I started elementary school. I made new friends with the boys in my class. They hated girls. They said they had cooties. I had no idea what cooties were, and thought my new friends were idiots. But still I needed friends while I was in school, even though they could never compare with my next-door neighbor, who happened to be a girl.

The next year Ginny started elementary school at the same school. She was so excited that her best friend was there to show her around, and so proud that she would be attending the same school I was. I was standing with a group of my "friends," the idiots who hated girls and thought they had some imagined disease. Ginny came running up to me, her arms open wide, so happy and excited to see me. She said she had been looking for me all morning, and now she had finally found me.

My friends looked at me in amazement and suspicion. What was this girl doing running up to their friend, a supposed fellow girl-hater, and hugging him? And then I made the first major mistake I was to make in my entire life, a mistake that has haunted me to this very day. To save face among those who were not my real friends, I turned away from the only real friend I had ever had. I pushed Ginny away and told her that she couldn't talk to me at school. And worse, I pretended I didn't even know her. She was devastated. I had broken the heart of my very best friend in the whole world.

Ginny didn't attend school for the next few days. Her parents said she was not to see me again. My heart was broken too. And I had broken it. I betrayed not only my very best and dearest friend, my future wife, but I betrayed myself. I chose a lie over truth. I chose fear over love. Even at age six, this was completely clear. Children are often far wiser and more connected to truth than adults. It would not be my last such mistake.

And this is how we move away from our True Self, from our True Being. We invest in lies instead of truth. We invest in fear instead of love. This is how it begins. In our culture we call this growing up, becoming mature, and later becoming adult. What it really is is betraying our True Self: betraying love.

I had carried the guilt of this first betrayal ever since then. So I knew it meant something. Pain is simply a lesson waiting to be learned. Until I just wrote this I did not know what it was. Now I think I do. Any betrayal of an apparent other is always really a betrayal of one's own self. When Ginny and I were lying in the tall grass, looking up at the clouds, our arms wrapped around each other or holding hands, we did not become one, we simply knew we were never not one. The learning of separation came later. It had already begun in a hundred ways, but it took a major step forward that day at school when I betrayed both Ginny and myself in that one cowardly and dishonest act.

For love is nothing but the absence of that illusory but stubborn sense of separation that becomes ever stronger as we move into adulthood. And the end of that imaginary sense of separation is the most wonderful thing a human can experience. If we look clearly and openly at our life, we will see that these lessons have always been here, just waiting for us to see

CHAPTER SEVEN

Falling in Love with Love

WHETHER WE'RE NOW IN LOVE or that is just a fond memory, we all love to fall in love. Can you think of a better time in your life than when you are in love? When we're with our Beloved, all problems fade. We're filled with peace, joy and love. This is as close to Heaven as most people ever experience while still in physical bodies. Our body seems so light we might as well be walking on clouds. You love your Beloved completely and your Beloved loves you just as much. What could be better?

The entire world takes on a different feel. It's as if the world itself has become lighter and filled with love. Is it any wonder that we love falling in love? To some of the more cynical in the world, falling in love can appear frivolous, unrealistic and unproductive. It can appear to be the delusional stage before the big letdown, when all this miraculous beauty comes crashing down and cold hard reality reasserts itself. And perhaps these more cynical folks might have had some bitter experiences that cause them to doubt the magical power of this state of being.

Those who no longer believe in the incredible, miraculous magic of love have closed their hearts to the truth of it. Because they did not truly understand what love is, they experienced hurt, suffering and pain. They then blamed this disappointment, caused by distorted and unrealistic expectations, on love itself. That was never the case. It was their misunderstanding of the nature of love that caused this disappointment and pain.

Those whose hearts are still open can see in their brothers and sisters that a life without love, a life lived through a closed heart, is not a life worth living at all. It is missing the very core and marrow of life. It is a life half lived at best. You can see it in the faces and body postures of those who have closed their hearts and live without love. And yet as soon as they fall in love, they come to life again. Their skin, which was once gray and shallow, appears to glow with an inner light. Their posture, which was once bent and hunched over, is now straight and strong. Where they shuffled there is now a spring in their step. Where there was only fear, judgment and death in their eyes, there is now life and love. Resurrection is possible. Love makes it possible. This is a miracle. But it is such a common miracle that it happens all the time. Anyone with eyes can see this.

And yet there are many who look down on the bliss of love, calling it unrealistic and delusional. They don't realize that it's their perception of life that's deluded. They hold their pain and suffering close inside their heart, no longer daring to even look at it. And so they have turned the glory of love into an experience of unacceptable pain and fear. This is the true distortion. And it is a great human tragedy. Yet there is always the opportunity to once again open their closed and protected heart. And it is only love itself that can do this.

A Course in Miracles says that there only two things in this world. One is love. The other is the call for love. And those who have tragically and mistakenly closed their hearts to love are at the same time desperately calling for love. For it is very clear, even to them, that a life without love is not a life worth living. So those who appear to have rejected love are actually desperately calling for love. They are like drowning people crying out for air.

The only correct response to such people is love – just as it is the only correct response for people whose hearts are open to love. In other words, the only correct response in any and every situation is love. Everyone you meet is either coming to you with a heart filled with love or with a cry for love. So your only correct response in either case is love.

It is true that when we do not understand love, the great bliss of falling in love does seem to change. It is not that we are finally facing reality that causes this change. It is that we have not completely seen through illusion yet. It is illusion that returns to take the place of love once again. Love is reality. Separation, fear and absence of love are the illusions.

Falling in love with love is not falling in love with a person. It is realizing this state of love itself as reality. Love encompasses and embraces all people, all beings, all of life. This is the truth of love. We begin to notice this with a special person. This person triggers our awareness and gives us permission to experience this basic truth of life. It's natural to attribute the experience of love to this very special person. This is beautiful, except that instead of realizing that this experience of love is actually the experience of reality, and this blissful state is always within us, we focus so much on the special person who granted us permission to experience our True Self that we miss the obvious fact that we in fact ARE this love. And this is where the pain and heartbreak can begin. If the other person is the sole and only source of this love and it is not ourselves, then we must become overly dependent on this very special person in order to experience who we truly are. And this is where the inevitable trouble and disappointment begins.

CHAPTER EIGHT

My Amazing Revelation at Sixteen

WHEN I WAS SIXTEEN I had a huge crush on Rachel, a beautiful young girl at my school. I had not asked her out yet. I was a bit nervous that she wouldn't accept. Her best friend approached me one day and told me Rachel had a huge crush on me and was hoping I would talk to her. Oh Happy Day! After school we went back to her house. We made out and did the things that teenagers in love do when not under the watchful eyes of their parents.

It took a little more than two hours for me to walk home. And I was walking on clouds. It was Spring, but it would have seemed like Spring no matter what the season was. The birds created a beautiful symphony. The sun reflected its brilliance off every leaf and freshly blooming flower. Every breeze testified I had been transported to the purest of Heavens.

And I was not the only one affected by this transformation. Adults, complete strangers, waved and smiled at me as they drove by. This never happened to me. Somehow what I was feeling also affected them. It made them happier. It changed the scruffy-looking teenager they usually avoided, condemned or feared into someone they loved. Could this be anything other than a miracle?

And it wasn't the last.

It was then I noticed it had been over an hour since I had been with Rachel. At this moment she was not with me, and still my heart was soaring and all of this was happening. How could this be? It was not just my memory or imagination of her. I was actually experiencing these things at this very moment. I suddenly realized that what I was experiencing did not come from her. It came from me. And not only that, it had always been here. It had always been right here in my heart. I just hadn't noticed it. It took this beautiful young girl to trigger my awareness of what had always been right here in my heart. At that moment, love took on a very different and far more expansive meaning.

I can't say I didn't forget this bit of insight soon after its discovery. I did, many times. But something from that day stayed with me. Something had awakened in me and could never be completely forgotten. You might even say that particular day, and countless events before and after, created this book you are holding in your hands. And you would not be wrong.

CHAPTER NINE

Love Cannot Cause Pain

PEOPLE WILL INEVITABLY DISAPPOINT. They are changeable. Love never disappoints. Love is not changeable. This is why falling in love with love itself is a better strategy for life and love. It does not mean you love this very special person less. You love more because your love is consistent, and without fear or need. If the special person does something you do not like, your love remains consistent. It does not change. This is because you love unconditionally.

The world is changeable. It is unreliable. Love is consistent and always reliable. The one who gives you permission to open your heart so fully that you realize yourself as love, and nothing but love, is a wonderful blessing in your life. He or she deserves all the love, honor and gratitude you give to them. But use this permission to realize who you truly are. Use this great gift to awaken to your True Self. Your True Self is love.

We ARE love. All that we see and experience is nothing but love. This is what it means to fall in love with love. When we fall in love, this happens naturally. We perceive that it is our Beloved that is the source of this feeling in us. And until we are ready to see deeper, this is fine. But I believe that for many of us, it is time for us to see deeper. It is time for us to realize who and what we really are. It is time for us to discover our True Self. Not as a belief, religious or otherwise, but as a direct, undeniable experience. And I have experienced in my own life that love is the way to do this. From the moment of my birth on Valentine's Day, love has shown me the way. Through intense heartbreak, abandonment and betrayal to wonderful loving relationships, I have not only learned everything of any value through love, but I have experienced the height of human value – which is to wake up from the dream of separation under which most of humanity still suffers.

So, My Dearest Love, Welcome Home. For when you turn within, when you move through the aches and pains that you imagine encase your heart, you will finally find True Love. You will find your True Self and the True Self of every person you encounter. You will find God. This is the end of suffering. This is awakening. It is a path you have been following without knowing it for a very long time, far beyond even this lifetime. And perhaps, as you read this, you are beginning to feel something stir within your heart, something that has lain hidden for a very long time. If this is so, I welcome you Home. And this is the true purpose of this book. It is only meant to awaken you, to arouse your sleeping Heart. If it is not happening yet, do not worry. It will. This is your path, just as it is mine. If your Heart does not awaken upon hearing these words, it will at another time and through another means. But it will awaken, My Dearest One. It will awaken. And the glory and majesty of such an awakening will make the very Heavens erupt in celebration. For you are my Dearest One. And I have been waiting for you to come Home. The time of imagined separation has served its purpose. All the suffering has served its purpose. Now it is time to return Home. You have never really left except in your imagination, except in this dream. Now it is time to return. If not now, then very soon. And I am waiting to embrace you.

Each day, more and more are awakening. The dream itself is dissolving. It has served its purpose. The purpose of the dream was only so that we could truly know our True Self by knowing its imagined opposite. And we have lived as this imagined opposite for a very long time. And now that time is over for you. Now you are coming Home – if not this moment, then soon, very soon. And for that I am so very grateful.

This longing that you feel deep down in your heart is only this emerging. It is only this calling to awaken to who you truly are. When you cry during a romantic movie, it is really only this longing calling to you. When you meet that certain special someone who rekindles the flame in your heart, it is only this deep longing calling you Home. All your life and the lives that came before, this has been happening. Right now you know this. Deep in your heart you know this. Your human mind may not know this, at least not yet, but your Divine Heart knows it intimately.

CHAPTER TEN

A Message of Love

I NEVER REALLY KNOW what I am writing. It just flows effortlessly in response to a certain need. It is as if some cosmic tap has been turned on full. I'm more like a typist trying to keep up. And there is no idea that a separate I, Peter, am writing to a separate other. It is simply fingers typing and one single Heart that is open everywhere at once, both giving and receiving at exactly the same time. And somehow these words that carry this energy need to manifest in this world. And none of it has ever been separate from anything else.

It's hard to resist it forever. Love is Truth. And the only real Truth there is is Love. Even the difficulties and resistance and ignorance are only ways of coming back to this one thing. Our entire lives are really only infinite ways of returning back to this one thing. We experience difficulties because we forget this Truth and act out of imagined separation. "I am different from you and have my own ideas and fears and goals that are different from yours." This we call conflict. But it too is only ignorance of this one Truth. It is simply a forgetting. And all the incredible pain and suffering that comes from this simple forgetting can also be used to point us Home again.

There are so many things to do to try and make the dream better, more comfortable, more perfect. End hunger. End war. Solve climate change. Create an enlightened society. But these things are all planned and done in the dream itself. So they can never be perfect. There will always be problems. There will always be suffering. That is the nature of the dream itself. It cannot be otherwise. If it were, if it were truly possible to make the dream perfect, then nobody would wake up. Why bother? The dream would also be perfect and, if it were, it would be much easier to simply stay in it rather than step into the complete unknown.

But it is not perfect. And those who are aware of this realize the suffering very deeply. So eventually, awakening becomes everything. And then it is inevitable. Until then, suffering will continue. That is the nature of the dream. And suffering is also the perfection of the dream. It alone is what leads us out of the dream.

The nature of reality is Love. Only this. Even in the dream we have glimmers of this. We are aware of the miracles that accompany Love. Love means the end of separation. That is all it means. And this feels very good. There is nothing that a separate human can experience that even comes close to this. We are not aware of this. We think it is about another person, a beloved, or a beloved teacher. We are not aware that it is Love itself that we are experiencing. It is the momentary shedding of all separation. And in this we are able to see beyond the thick, seemingly impenetrable, imagined walls of the dream. And it is quite glorious. So we want more. This too is a very natural impulse to awaken. There is both pain and suffering (the stick) and the wonders of falling in love (the carrot). Both are leading us Home.

My advice is to have faith in this alone. Only Love. That will burn up all sense of separation. It is very powerful. When even one person experiences this deeply, the entire group, no matter how large, seems to get a taste and moves closer to awakening, closer to non-separation, closer to Love. Not even a word needs to be spoken by this one person. This has been my experience. It is quite miraculous.

The mind will never understand this. It is not of the mind.

And the mind is incapable of understanding it. The mind is born of the belief in separation and can only serve this. This is understood only in the Heart. Compared to the mind, it is a very silent place. It doesn't have much to say. And mostly it speaks in silence. But what it speaks is immensely powerful. Only the Heart is capable of understanding the absence of all separation.

CHAPTER ELEVEN

Falling in Love with Truth

TO HAVE GREAT RELATIONSHIPS, first fall in love with Truth. You may also call it Love or God if you like, but for now Truth will do. The spiritual teacher Gangaji says that the source of her beautiful relationship with her husband comes from their commitment to put their love of Truth first above all other things, including each other and their relationship. In this way their relationship is about something greater than themselves. And this is the great secret of beautiful relationships.

When I speak of Truth, people are often confused. They ask me, "Whose truth? Yours or mine?" They believe that everyone has their own truth. What they mean is not Truth, but belief or opinion. Beliefs and opinions are called relative truths. And yes indeed: every single person has their own relative truth. They have their own relative truths that they completely believe are real and true. At least until they change into other truths. Relative truths change. They evolve when new knowledge or experiences come into our lives.

Truth with a capital "T" is not like this. Truth with a capital "T" we might call ultimate truth, as opposed to relative truth. Truth with a capital "T" is not your truth or my truth. It does not change. It is not a belief or an opinion. What may be even harder to grasp for the mind is that Truth with a capital "T" cannot even really be described. It cannot be grasped with the mind. It simply is. And that is enough.

So how do you fall in love with something that cannot be described or understood with the mind? That's a good question. The best I can offer is that you simply do. When you taste ultimate Truth, you cannot help but fall in love with it. It is not separate from Love itself. You may notice that I also use a capital "L" for love to indicate unconditional love, not conditional love. When all your relative truths, your beliefs and opinions about life and who you are, about everything you ever held a belief and opinion about, are surrendered, then ultimate Truth with a capital 'T' is simply here. You might even say that ultimate Truth is simply you, who you really are, in complete harmony with all of life, not separate from any particle of existence, the absolute freedom of pure spirit. Any verbal description must be lacking in the direct experience. And ultimate Truth is the experience, the beingness, not any mental knowledge you can store away. It is alive. It is present. It is here and now.

You have experienced a taste of ultimate Truth whenever you have felt truly happy, whenever you have felt completely free, and when you fall in love. In each of these experiences you are no longer in opposition to the universe. You are no longer in opposition to anything or anyone. You are in harmony. The ordinary separation of the ego has faded and you are One with All That Is. In these moments, you taste ultimate Truth. It's impossible to really describe what that experience is like. As soon as you do, you return to the mind and the mind must create separation in order to understand and describe. It must create an object that the subject can grasp. And ultimate Truth is not an object. It's not a thought, a feeling, an opinion or belief. It's not an object of any kind. It's simply what it is: Truth, the Truth of you, the Truth of All That Is.

You could also call this "falling in love with enlightenment." Falling in love with Truth, your True Self, Love, enlightenment, God – all point to the same thing. It is beyond words, so words can only be pointers to the direct experience. When you fall in love with ultimate Truth, or whichever word pointers you want to use, you will put this first in your life. You will no longer say, "I have a very busy week, but this weekend I plan to spend some time on enlightenment." Twenty-four hours a day, seven days a week, this will always be your main concern. While you are working, while you are eating, while you are making love, while you are sleeping, ultimate Truth will be with you – and now you will be aware of it. This is how you fall in love with Truth.

And this falling in love with Truth will permeate your life and all of your relationships. No longer will your relationship with your Beloved, or even your Beloved, come first. Now it will always be ultimate Truth. And this will bring the all-important unconditional love to your relationship. It will create new eyes and a new heart from which you now perceive your Beloved. You will see everything and everyone with the eyes of Love, the eyes of Truth. You will live in peace, love and joy, in harmony with all of life.

All of this will not happen at once. It's a journey. What is not Truth, what is not unconditional Love, must be shed. And this will happen as long as Truth always comes first in your life. When the illusory relative truths have priority, your life will continue to be about these illusions. And you will continue suffering. When ultimate Truth has priority, then what is not ultimate Truth will gradually fade away. You will notice freedom, peace, love and happiness filling your life more and more. These are the perfumes of ultimate Truth. The more the false is shed and Truth embraced, the more present this wonderful perfume will be.

To fall in love with Truth, start where you are. Where else could you start? It's a decision you can make right now. No preparation is needed. Spiritual practice is all about surrender. Surrender what is false so what is True can be seen. Nothing can change Truth. It remains always what it is. Yet it can be hidden from our view by false conditioned thoughts. And these thoughts can be about anything, even God, Truth, enlightenment or Love. The mind will never understand ultimate Truth. It is not an object. It is not something that can be grasped or understood. It is simply by shedding all thoughts, including thoughts about ultimate Truth, that ultimate Truth is revealed as always being right here and now. You cannot gain or attain ultimate Truth. It is far more accessible than that. It has never been separate from what you really are. And you have never been separate from It.

If you want to fall in love, fall in love with ultimate Truth. Right now you love many things. You have preferences for one thing or person and reject another. You have many logical reasons for your preferences. And some of these reasons are deeply unconscious. Ultimate Truth is beyond any preferences or logical reasons. It is beyond all your unconscious thoughts as well. It sees no differences anywhere. In this way, ultimate Truth and unconditional Love are the same. They are both not separate from what you are. So you could also say that falling in love with Truth is falling in love with the Self. I won't say your Self because nobody owns this Self. This Self is what you are. It is what everything is.

It can be challenging to really love yourself as a limited separate self. You make positive affirmations about how loveable and wonderful you are. And deep in your unconscious are the repressed thoughts that are saying the exact opposite. It never seems to really work out completely. But the True Self that you are is Love itself. It is absolutely impossible not to be completely in love with the Self. It takes no effort or positive affirmations at all. As soon as you recognize the Self, you are filled to the brim with love. Love and the Self cannot be separated.

Whatever name you want to give it, fall in love with ultimate Truth. Begin where you are and make this the number-one priority in your life. Love Truth so much that everything that is not Truth dissolves in the powerful light of Truth. The title of this book – *The Zen of Love* – also refers to this ultimate Truth. Unconditional Love is not separate from ultimate Truth. Neither can be understood with the human mind. Both are experienced in the Heart. And this Heart is not limited to a place in your body. It is everywhere. And so are You.

CHAPTER TWELVE

Being Awake

I, AS THE PERSON PETER, am not awake. I cannot be, as a person. The person Peter does not dream he is awake. But, as love itself, which does not even know or acknowledge the person Peter, I am very much awake.

This may appear confusing. So simply, as love itself, without any person, past, history, or anything other than love itself, love itself is awake. It is awake to itself as love itself. And that is all it can be awake to, and all that being awake means. It means the entire world is nothing but love.

There is no separate person. There are no others. There is only love. And this is what I feel. And this is what I experience. I can believe that I am Peter again and act as such. But it is not a belief or act that I favor or enjoy very much. I do still enjoy it a little in small doses. Peter is a wonderful persona or mask or illusion. He is very loving and kind and reasonably wise as personas go. But this is not really what I am. I have no name, no form, no shape or size, no limits, no boundaries, no past, no future, no present, no beginning and no end. And this realization is what it truly means to be awake.

The rest is playing in the dream. And it is fine to play in the dream until you no longer want to. It is perfectly fine. It is perfect. You will play in the dream as the dream exactly as long as you need to. This is very good. You can play as anything you want to play as and need to play as for your learning. There is nothing wrong with the dream. It is completely necessary.

Until it no longer is. When it no longer is, we become extraordinarily focused. We only want Truth. We only want to wake up. We have absolutely no other desires in the entire world. You might say we become a very boring person. We are only interested in one thing, to the exclusion of the entire world. We want this more than we want our own life. We would give up our own life for this. And more than a few are close to suicide before they finally wake up. Our own life actually becomes entirely meaningless and we lose all interest in it. The dream may even begin to appear transparent, as if we can see right through it.

Our only focus is waking up, whatever that means, because we really have no idea what that means. Even after we wake up it's nothing we can really define in words, although we know it completely, just not in any mental, thought-based way. It is a direct experience, and beyond all words.

I do still teach, heal, write, and more. But it is not really me as Peter who does this. The dream of Peter is not really capable of doing these things, or at least not very well. Not as I do them now. Something quite profound happens. Peter is just going along for the ride as sort of a form that people can identify with. What I really am is Love itself. People who believe themselves to be people can not identify with this consciously, although unconsciously they do so very much. Many believe they love me. But what they are always seeing and loving is love itself. Which is none other than what they are themselves. All writing, teaching and healing only point back to this same thing, over and over and over again. I have nothing else to say. I have nothing new to say. This is what I am. This is all I really know.

And yet I continue to act in the dream, more or less as a person. I just don't believe it as others do. Although I sometimes still forget. The dream still has a little momentum left. And that is where suffering is very useful. Suffering is the vehicle we use to come back to Truth. It shows us where we have forgotten who we are. It is nothing but a reminder. While we still believe in the dream it seems very real and important. But it is nothing but a reminder. It can go on for a very long time if we don't remember. And this is also perfect. A limited separate self will always suffer. It is its nature. And you might also say it is its expiration date. Because it can, and does for some, expire before the limited body/mind does. We call this "dying before you die." We also call it waking up. It is wonderful, the most wonderful thing a human can experience. This limited, separate self is just a dream. Who you truly are can never suffer. Who you truly are can never die. It is love itself. How can that suffer? How can that die? It is and can only experience love.

I know that's a lot to take in. Don't worry about it. You will only take in exactly what you need to, exactly when you need to. The True You is completely taking care of everything, all the time. The True You is teaching you in the dream all the time. Everything that happens in the dream is teaching you. Just as your sleeping dreams are teaching you. It is a wonderful school, 24/7. You could not find a better school or teacher anywhere in the universe. This is something to be extremely grateful for. You are love itself. So you can only treat and take care of yourself as love itself. You have no other way. Yes, there is pain and suffering involved in these extremely loving and generous lessons. That is part of the lesson. That is pointing out for you to see the dream in the clearest way, in the way most guaranteed to get your full attention. If you were truly a limited, separate person, then it would feel like this. Do you like this experience of suffering? No? Then see if it is actually real. Take a closer look.

When you experience great peace, love or joy, see what this is really pointing to. Is it really coming from some person or situation out there – a grandchild, husband, winning the lottery? Or is the peace, love or joy actually occurring right here inside? And, just maybe, has it been right here all along but you just haven't noticed? Just maybe, you have been looking outside for something that you have in fact always actually been?

Your True Self is always guiding you back home. It will appear outside as teachers, friends, lovers, children, situations – whatever you need it to appear as. But it has never ever been other than what it is. It is so beautiful, so generous, so loving. It is always acting. It appears as anything or anyone you need it to. But it is never other than what you truly are. In the dream, this sounds crazy. We are individual separate beings in a world of individual separate beings. But that is really just a dream. Just imagination. Just thoughts and beliefs. Really there is only this True Self, this One True Self, this One True Heart, this One True Love. And that is what I am. And that is what you are. The realization, the conscious awake knowing of this, is what we call being awake.

CHAPTER THIRTEEN

The Story of My Awakening

THERE ARE MANY who have expressed an interest in the story of my awakening and how it happened. It is not the easiest story to tell, because there was not one sudden brilliant flash and then it was done. It was a series of progressive insights, punctuated by occasional big leaps that began pretty much at birth and continued on. And it is still continuing.

Eckhart Tolle's story is one of a single, incredibly powerful and transformative night. Mine is not like that, although there have been times when I wished it were. But I no longer do. Why has my journey been one of slow, gradual and progressive awakenings? It has been for you. It has been entirely for you.

In fact the story of my awakening is not, as is commonly thought, all about me. It is instead not about me at all, but about you. This is extremely important to understand, so I'm telling you this right at the start. It is very dangerous and distracting to focus on the events in anyone's story and imagine that these same things need to happen to you if you are to awaken yourself. Comparisons are not productive. Each of us awakens in our own time and our own way. It is already happening for you right now, whether you are aware of it or not. And it is happening in a way that is exactly perfect for you. This is very important to understand.

It may be interesting to read the awakening stories of others.

And these stories can be inspiring and motivating. They can open your heart and mind to what is possible. They can help you see beyond the veil of separation. But these are all simply stories. They too are merely appearances in a dream. What they each point to is already happening in you. And this is the most important thing: this inner unfolding and awakening that is happening right now in you in its own absolutely perfect way.

If I were to tell my story of awakening simply to impress you and make me out to be special and separate from you, what would be the point? What possible value could you really gain from this? It may be slightly interesting, a curiosity, a form of momentary entertainment. But ultimately, it would simply be another distraction from who you really are. And we all have enough of those already. Instead, I want you to see beyond the details to what this story and all stories of awakening point to. And that is your own awakening.

What you will read in this story may be familiar to you or completely unfamiliar. You may have experienced similar things or find some of the events incomprehensible, far out or unbelievable. It does not matter. This has been my experience of awakening. You will have your own completely and perfectly unique experiences. In fact, you already are having them. How do I know you are awakening? Trust me, I do. For this apparent separation between you and me, between writer and reader, is not real. What you are experiencing I also experience. Not only as you are reading this in some sort of psychic bond, but always and in much more than a psychic bond. We are One, you and I. Just now you may not yet be consciously aware of this. But you will be. This is your inner unfolding, your inner awakening. And it has already begun.

As you will see in my story, the unfolding into this realization was a gradual one, very much like what is happening in you. The details may seem very different. But this story, our story, is not about the details, interesting as they might be. It is about something much deeper, and not always easily seen.

The Story of My Awakening - How It Began

I will begin this story not at the beginning, but at my birth or soon after my birth in a physical body. As a young child I was blessed to live in a house surrounded by many acres of forest. My father's love of nature flowed into me and I spent much of every day out in this forest, often alone. When I was alone, undistracted by conversation, the forest came truly alive for me. Through a young child's eyes, every tree, rock, leaf and twig danced with an inner energy and spirit. I felt at one with this forest and everything within it. There may have been turmoil, confusion and suffering within the house, but the forest was a place of refuge for a young child. It was magical, sacred and holy. And it was safe.

Sitting alone in the forest – in this peace, safety and refuge – my mind would naturally quiet, and I would feel filled with light and love. Later, when I learned the word God, I thought of it as being filled with the Presence of God. I didn't know how many other children experienced this, if any at all. I did realize that nobody talked about it. So I never told another soul about this until I was ten years old. It was very personal, and somehow I thought it best to keep it that way.

My family was not religious and never talked about God or religion, another reason for me to keep these experiences to myself. Once a year, on Christmas Eve, my mother would take us to church. When I was ten, the minister at the church took an interest in me. He probably knew something of the drinking and other problems that were going on in my home. He convinced my mother to bring me to church each Sunday, where I would be an acolyte and help him with the services. He must have been very convincing, because in spite of severe hangovers, she did it for almost a year. This minister was the first person I told about my experiences with the "Presence of God." He understood exactly what I was experiencing, and he encouraged me. He had experienced and still did experience the same thing. He called it his "calling." He said it was why he had become a minister.

Please don't get the impression that I was always experiencing this "Presence of God" as a child. Most of the time I was not. Most of the time I experienced quite a lot of suffering, separation and fear, possibly more than most children who might have had a more stable home life. But I did have this refuge. I didn't know how to control it. It just happened when I was alone in what I considered a safe place, like the forest, and later in the church when it was empty.

For quite some time I felt as though I was living a double life. On the surface I was a relatively "normal" boy, interested in sports, movies, monsters and mischief. And underneath this was the secret life that still felt the Presence of God, and had become fascinated with Saint Francis of Assisi. Except for my church minister, there was nobody I would dare tell about that side of my life. I felt very sure they would not understand. So I continued leading a double life.

When I was twelve years old, I took on a new interest. Or maybe it might be more accurate to say a new interest took me over. And it really did take me over fairly completely. Sex. Girls. That became my whole life. I hooked up with a wise, independent and experienced fourteen-year-old girl and had my initiation. I don't think there was anything I thought about after that that was not connected to sex in some way or other. Art and music, success, fame were really just other ways to get more sex.

At that point, I no longer experienced the Presence of God consciously for quite some time. The secret life of God faded away from my consciousness. The life of the world became everything. And most of that centered around sex. I became hyper aware of my body, not only as a way to experience and give pleasure, but also as a form of attraction to members of the opposite sex. I became firmly identified with the body and what it did. The interest in Saint Francis, God and monkhood faded so far into the background that it was no longer noticed at all. I developed a bad boy, rebel persona. It wasn't just that my home life was pretty rocky; it seemed to attract more girls. I fit into certain teenage categories or groups, first as a juvenile delinquent, then as a hippie rock-and-roller.

Contrary to popular belief, forgetting about God and getting lost in sex, body identity and the world was not slipping backwards away from God. It too was all part of the process of awakening itself. There is nothing that happens in your life that is not part of the awakening process. Even if you feel you are slipping backwards or getting lost, do not worry. This too is an essential part of your awakening. Everything is always going perfectly, no matter what you think or perceive is happening.

By nineteen I already had two children, two beautiful, angelic twin daughters. After they were born I took up yoga and meditation, mostly to stop using drugs. It didn't seem right to be using drugs when I had these two innocent angel beings with me. The inner call to God was beginning to reassert itself. It just happened to show up in the form of these two, tiny, perfect little angels.

At twenty-two, as a complete surprise to me, I completely woke up. I had mostly forgotten about God and become completely immersed in the world by this time. I was struggling to make a name for myself as an artist and photographer. My mother, an alcoholic and pill addict, was in another alcohol and drug rehabilitation program. This one was in Florida. During the last week of the program, they invited family members to attend – to help educate us about addiction and living with an addict, and to help create a smooth transition for the addict back into "normal" life. Although I had not lived with my mother for many years, my brother and I agreed to do this in hopes that it might help. Also, it was a free trip to Florida in the winter, which is very appealing if you live in the Northeast. I had no idea it would be part of a full-blown awakening that would forever change the course of my life.

Sitting in daily meetings where adult alcoholics shared the

depths of their experiences of hitting bottom did not fill me with understanding and compassion. Just the opposite. They filled me with rage. My mother's alcoholism had created enough suffering in the lives of my brother, sister and me. Some of these people were even worse. One man had been the Chief of Surgery in a major New York hospital. His addiction to alcohol and various pills was so severe that his hands would shake uncontrollably in the middle of surgeries. He admitted that a number of patients had died on his operating table because of this. Because he was Chief of Surgery, the nurses and other staff covered up for him. Listening to this story, I was seething with anger. It was bad enough that these people had destroyed the lives of their children as well as themselves, but this man had committed murder and gotten away with it. I was so angry I didn't think I could continue in the program.

That night everything changed.

For reasons I still can't explain, the angry, judgmental person I thought I was completely disappeared. My body or any identification with my body completely disappeared. All that was left was light, and infinite, overwhelming unconditional love. It is impossible to describe how good this felt. I was no longer separate from anything. Where I had felt anger and judgment toward my mother and the other alcoholics, now all I could feel was the most perfect and unconditional love. The person Peter had been replaced with love. And this complete transformation didn't affect only me. It affected every person I came in contact with.
The alcoholics, their family members and even the counselors were drawn to this scruffy, twenty-two-year-old hippie like moths to a bright light. I said very little, but I was emanating a very powerful and magnetic light, the light of unconditional love. One at a time, they approached me and poured their hearts out to me. I didn't even need to hear what they spoke. I

could see their entire lives from the moment of their birth. I knew them completely and I loved them completely and unconditionally. I don't remember what I said to anyone. But being with me was clearly very healing for them.

And I probably don't need to say how healing it was for me. Where only a day before I had been so enraged at the Chief of Surgery, now I could instantly see his entire life, and experience each moment as if it were mine – because it is. Everything made complete sense. Every act was inevitable and perfect. I loved every perfect bit of it and I loved him unconditionally. All imagined separation between us had dissolved completely. As he rested his head on my shoulder, sobbing uncontrollably, I held him like a beloved child and I began to understand the power of love to heal.

How or why this happened I cannot say. I barely even knew the word Enlightenment. I had read Siddhartha. I had been practicing yoga and a little meditation for a few years. But I really don't think that had anything to do with this huge, sudden shift. Because these things can't really be understood with the human mind, we might simply call it Grace. It needed to happen – so it did.

You might never experience such a sudden shift in your life, and that does not matter. You might not have experienced what I called the Presence of God in your early years. It makes no difference. The process of awakening is happening in you perfectly, just as it did in me. It is happening in your own unique way, just as it must. Trust this.

This sudden awakening in my early twenties only lasted for about ten days. It wasn't just the people in the rehab center who were drawn to me for healing. Everywhere I went, this happened. And then after ten days, this incredible light, love and bliss began to fade. That's what it felt like. After I returned home, the familiar environment triggered the egoic personality to reassert itself. My wife, friends and neighbors expected and wanted the old Peter back again. And after a while, they got it.

I had no idea how I entered into this awakened state. And I had even less of an idea how I left it. That was the beginning of my spiritual search. I spent the next forty years trying to get back to a place that, without my knowing it, I could never have left. I spent the next forty years trying to get Home, without realizing I could never be anyplace else.

The seeming fading of this awakened state was just as perfect as its appearance, as was the long and often frustrating journey to rediscover it. The egoic personality needed to spin itself out. It needed to show all its tricks. It needed to accomplish many of the things it believed would bring it happiness and love: fame, wealth, relationships, sex, success. It needed to gain these things so it could very directly experience their emptiness and become disillusioned. It needed to experience all of this in the dream to make the next awakening solid and mature. And it needed to do this for you.

Along this imagined journey there were many mini-awakenings to keep the path fresh and alive. And none of it was done by the personal egoic self. Some people use the word Grace, because really we don't know. We don't really know why or how we awaken. Just as we don't know why or how we entered the dream of a separate self. We don't really know much of anything. It's good to admit this from time to time. It's good to be aware of this all the time.

You may wonder if I healed my mother during this experience. The answer is no, in terms of her alcoholism. As with all the others, I could see her entire life. What I saw was that she was terrified of intimacy. She was terrified of love. Can you imagine being terrified of, and resisting, the one thing that all humans crave above everything else? Is it surprising that someone would spend their life drunk or on drugs if this is how they feel? The experience may not have healed her, but it certainly healed me. My anger was turned to understanding, compassion and love. And that remained with me even when the awakened consciousness seemed to fade.

At some point I realized that everything in my life had really been leading me Home. I mean that literally. Every single thing I experienced in my life was always leading me Home. This is why I say today that everything happens for my benefit. It doesn't matter what it is, it is always only happening for my benefit. And I will say, if you let me, that this is also true of you. This is as true of cancer, which I had ten years ago, as it is of the miraculous healing from cancer that came a few years later. This is also when I discovered that love was not only my path to Enlightenment, but was Enlightenment itself.

Since everything in life from the moment of my birth was always leading me Home, was always awakening me, I will not bore you with every single detail of my life. The ones that are relevant to you, I will include in parts of this book, and in other teachings and in healing if they are useful

Please remember that whatever you read about the awakening experiences of other people, it is only your own awakening that is important. Please remember this. Your own awakening is already happening. It has been happening since you first entered this dream world. You did not enter this dream without a trail of breadcrumbs leading you safely back out. You spread the breadcrumbs perfectly, and you will discover them just as perfectly. Perhaps this book may help you notice a few of them.

CHAPTER FOURTEEN

The Heart Song

WE'VE ALL FELT IT. We've all experienced it. When you look at your child playing in the grass on a summer's day. When a dear friend holds your hand in a time of great trouble. When you see a glorious sunset. When your new puppy wags his tail and scampers to you as soon as you come in the door. When you gaze into the eyes of your beloved as you finish making love. How can you say the world is not filled with love?

You may say, what about all the stories you hear on the news about war, poverty, crime, violence and corruption? The world does not always seem filled with love. It often seems filled with anything but.

Can these be anything but a deep call for love? Look into your own heart more deeply. Look deeply with me and see if your only real desire is for anything but love. You may say it is for fame, wealth, security, a stable relationship you can count on, the welfare of your children, or many other things that don't seem to be a call for love. But is this really true? Are not all these simply a call for your heart's one true desire? Are not these too only a call for love?

Can the desire for fame be other than so that people will love you? What other reason could there be? Is not your desire for wealth simply because you don't now feel loved or lovable enough and believe perhaps wealth will grant you this love? Did you know that some of the wealthiest people are also among the loneliest people on this earth? They are abundant in material resources, but in their hearts they feel starved for love. And this is why they continue to pursue more and more wealth, even at the expense of their health and their family. No matter how much money they make, it cannot buy what is already free and available to all. So seeking wealth is just another way to hide this feeling of emptiness and worthlessness that comes when you don't feel truly loved.

All this, you think you want. Yet all of this is really only a deep yearning for love. This is all your heart yearns for. This is your only true desire.

Some of us, perhaps you too, have carefully covered over this one true desire with other imagined goals. You have created substitute goals. It is just too painful to feel you are not loved, or even unworthy of love. You may feel that you are not loved the way you want to feel loved. Somehow it is not complete enough. It is not full enough. It is not real enough.

Oh, My Dear One, we have all felt this pain at one time or another. I know just how you feel. And I have felt this pain too. But this is not you. This is not your True Heart. So I have wonderful news for you. Your heart has never been empty of love, not for one single moment in your entire life. You have always been loved, and your heart has always been bursting to overflowing with the most precious thing the world has ever known. You may not believe this yet.

For so long, you have not understood love. You have suffered under the misunderstanding and mistaken ideas of love that are so common in human culture. You have seen it as small and limited. You have seen love as something you need to get or give. And in giving, you only had a limited supply that could run out. So you had to be very careful with your heart. You had to be very careful with such a limited supply of love. But love has never been like that. You thought that only the lucky few could achieve the love you craved so desperately. You did not understand that love can never be like that. It is as present as the air you breathe. It is carried on every breeze. It lives in every molecule that has ever existed. It lives in every cell of your precious body. Every star that shines in the night sky is expressing nothing but love. And you yourself are nothing but love. In fact, that is all you really are. And that is true of everyone else you see. Right now, love is dancing in your breath. When you breathe, you are breathing not air but love. It's delicious, isn't it? Could you ever imagine that simply breathing could feel so wonderful? And this is the magic of love. Whatever love touches creates miracles. And love touches everything. You just may not have noticed this before. But after reading this book, perhaps you will. Perhaps, like me, you will learn to see love everywhere.

CHAPTER FIFTEEN

An Exercise in Love and Awakening

> No one looks for stars when the sun is out. A person blended into God does not disappear. He or she is just completely soaked in God's qualities.
>
> – Rumi

LOVE IS WHAT WE ARE. It is all around us. We are love, swimming in a sea of love. But we think we are merely a tiny wave floating on top of this great ocean. This has never been true. But our thoughts are very convincing. And some of these thoughts lie beyond our conscious mind. They may have begun when we were just babies, before we even had words for what we were feeling. Or they were so painful that we repressed them, and they still continue on in our subconscious.

Before we begin with this exercise it's important to understand why this exercise is even necessary. Since you are love existing only in love, why would you need any exercise or practice to experience what already is? The reason is that you are resisting the truth of this. In your mind you have some very strong beliefs telling you that what you truly are is not true. These false thoughts present an alternative and very limited view of what is true. And this limited view is what you believe.

It may have begun when you were only an infant in diapers before you understood human language. Infants are still psychic because they have not yet developed the filters that separate them from others. Your mother or father may have been changing your diaper when you had a particularly unappealing poop. A momentary thought drifted through their mind about how disgusting this was, and for just a second they questioned whether having a child was such a good idea. Because you had not developed filters yet, you heard this thought and the feeling that went along with it. And in that moment you didn't feel as lovable as you did just a moment before. Later experiences built on this one, and you began to feel that you were only conditionally lovable. You were lovable when you behaved in certain ways, and not lovable when you behaved in others. None of this is true, but you began to believe it. So to your mind it became true. For most of us these thoughts are unconscious, and that makes them harder to be aware of, uproot and dissolve.

So thoughts continue to build up, one on top of another. Each thought reinforces the last thought. We begin to perceive life through these thoughts, and we become convinced that life is reinforcing these thoughts as true, when it is really only our thoughts that we perceive. We don't think to question whether the initial thought, or any of the other thoughts, are actually true. Whether they are conscious or unconscious, we believe in them completely.

And this is how we take what is unlimited and imagine that it is limited. We feel lovable, but only if we earn that love. We develop deep feelings of guilt, unworthiness, insecurity and a feeling that if people really knew us they would not love us. Most of these thoughts and feelings are repressed and lie beneath our conscious thinking – and no wonder. Who would ever consciously think thoughts like these? These are the thoughts with which we create our sense of personhood, of the unique, separate individual we believe is who we are. And so we naturally experience suffering. We feel that life, at best, has its good moments and bad moments. Sometimes we even experience love as being painful. Sometimes we believe that love is so painful that subconsciously we do our best to avoid it even though consciously we seem to seek it. All of these thoughts are pure illusion with not a shred of truth to them. But that doesn't matter, as long as we believe they are true. And such is the human condition.

It's true that we do experience love and joy at least occasionally, even if only temporarily. If we pay attention to those moments of love and joy, we realize that something is missing – those illusory thoughts of a separate person. We feel connected. We feel free. We feel One.

And this is why practices like meditation, and exercises such as the one I'm going to introduce you to shortly, are important. Their purpose is not to add anything new to your life, but only to strip away what is not true. When what is not true has been seen through and dissolved, what is true and what is always here will be revealed. If you did not carry these illusions about life and who you are, there would be no need for these practices or for any spiritual teaching at all. Their only purpose is to dissolve illusions so that the truth that is always here can be revealed. And that's what this exercise is for.

An Exercise in Love

Feel love. Feel this experience you know as love. Begin wherever you are right now. If you are in a love relationship now, feel your love for your Beloved. If you are not, feel your love for a past Beloved, a child, a pet, a friend or a parent. Take your time and simply allow this feeling of love to emerge. Remember, you're not adding anything here. You're simply revealing what already is.

Feel love. Allow this love to grow. What you may be feeling right now is probably very limited. That's because you're resisting what is already here, what is always here. You do not know this yet. Your beliefs in limitation and separation are still too strong. So I say ALLOW. Simply allow. Allow what is already here to emerge in your awareness.

You may experience fear, unworthiness, insecurity, guilt and the pain these feelings create. You may experience the memories of past heartbreaks. You may experience deep feelings of unlovability, even self-hatred. That is fine. That is to be expected. This is what your resistance is made of. Don't be frightened away.

Look at it. Feel it. Allow it. Now love it. Yes, love this too. Love what you have been repressing and resisting all your life. Shine this same love you felt for your Beloved on these painful feelings. Watch what happens when you do this. Notice how the painful feelings are dissolving in this love. This is because love is true. And none of those painful feelings are true. When you stop repressing them and allow them, accept them and love them, they reveal themselves as what they are and have always been. They have never been anything but thoughts. They never had any substance or reality. When they are seen through the light of Truth, which is not separate from love, they simply return to what they are – just a thought. And they fade away as all thoughts do. Your belief in them as something real and true has kept them alive and active all this time. Now that you finally see them as what they are, which happens automatically and effortlessly, they no longer have your belief and so they simply dissolve. They fade away as all thoughts do, and with them all the pain you have associated with them. They have no reality. What remains is love, because love is true. This is a wonderful exercise and a beautiful experience. Who would not want to exchange pain for love? Now you can do exactly that.

Experience Love Growing

You may have to do this many times before your resistance dissolves enough to allow love to reveal itself more than as the limited experience you're used to. Notice that each time you allow, accept and love a painful feeling until it dissolves, your experience of love grows. Love is always unlimited, infinite and eternal. It is only your experience of it that is limited. And that is only due to your resistance. As your resistance melts away, you experience more of the love that is always here.

At first you will need to make some effort to allow, accept and love these painful feelings you have repressed for so long. It is contrary to how you have lived your life up until this point. You are developing a new habit to take the place of the old one. Once you experience how effective it is, you will be motivated to continue. At a certain point, love will take over and effort will no longer be needed. Painful, illusory feelings always dissolve in the light of love, as you are already beginning to see. And when the awareness of love is strong enough, they no longer arise at all, just as darkness cannot exist in light.

Continue allowing love to grow. Remember it is really only your awareness of what is already here that is growing. But it will feel as if it is growing. Surrender to this love. It will soon feel as if your heart cannot contain this much love. Don't worry. It cannot. Simply allow it to spread past your heart and fill your entire body. The body cannot contain it either. Your awareness of this will grow at its own pace. Just allow it.

The Realization

As you continue dissolving all resistance, and surrendering to love, you will come to experience that there is nothing but love. It is like the air you are breathing. It is everywhere. Your feeling of separation from other people and eventually from all things will begin to dissolve. Your feeling of being a separate person will begin to dissolve. The wave has realized it has always been the ocean. Just bask in this true bliss. Take a few moments right now to just enjoy it. Now you know who you are. You are love. You are not separate from anything. The world of apparent separation can go on. Things appear to come and go. Your body itself will also go. But you are no longer fooled. You are unlimited, infinite and eternal. You are love, swimming in a sea of love. There is no separation between you and the sea. Enjoy. Be Happy. Welcome Home.

CHAPTER SIXTEEN

All There Is Is Love

THE ONLY THING THAT IS REAL in the world is love. And this is what is true. You may believe that it is not true. But love is really all there is. You may have suffered abuse, disease, death, and all manner of suffering. But is this really true? It certainly seems that way, doesn't it? It certainly seems as if suffering exists. You have felt it. You have felt your heart break in two. You have felt your life fall apart. You have felt fear, even terror. You have felt great sadness and despair. You have experienced momentary happiness, only to be plunged soon after into despair or anger, jealousy or grief. And this has been your world. This has been what you see, what you experience and what you know. This is what you perceive as the world and your life. And here I am, telling you that all of this is a lie, a misunderstanding, a confusion. I am saying that none of it is true. How can I say this? What does that mean to you? How can everything you have experienced all of your life not be true?

Buddha calls the life we believe is real an illusion. Jesus said much the same thing. All spiritual teachers have said that the world is a dream. And I too say that this is so. It is a dream. It is an illusion. I say that because I know that all there is is love. And yet, that is not what you see. You see war, poverty, disaster and death. You see violence and injustice. You see environmental devastation. You see all manner of suffering. But I do not see this. All I see is love. How can this be? Am I insane? Am I deluded, hallucinating or just incredibly stupid to see only love where you see cruelty, despair, homelessness and all manner of suffering? No, My Beloved One. I am not insane. Although when I saw the world as you now do, I was quite insane. I saw as you did. I saw all the despair and suffering you do. And this is how I know the insanity of seeing the world in this way. You must look very closely to see that there is only love. You must look not only with your eyes and your mind, but you must look mostly with your heart. You must look through the Eyes of Love. And I will teach you how to see in this way. I will teach you how to love. Because you are dearest to my heart, My Love. And because I love you, utterly, completely and unconditionally. And this is the truth of who and what you are. You are love itself. And so is everything you see and perceive.

Please notice when cracks appear in the illusion that you call the world, the illusion that you call your life. Please notice the moments of kindness, the moments of beauty, the moments of grace that shine on you in each and every moment. You may not notice them now – but trust me, they are here for you. Yes, each and every day, Grace shines on you. Love shines on you. Each and every day, this is what happens in your real life. You may miss them: the loving glance of stranger, the whisper of the wind in the trees, the sun shining on your face, the sudden joyous laugh of a child. Can there be anything but love in these things? Look at a sunset. Really look, My Dearest One. Can this be other than love?

Now you are getting the picture, I hope. Now you are beginning to see what I see. The world is a glorious symbol for love, a symbol for God in each and every thing there is. Even what you now consider bad or unpleasant or painful, which you usually run from or repress, is really only love. It is not coming in disguise. You have simply hidden its true meaning from yourself. If you see the world as love, you cannot continue with the dream you have created for yourself. So you must hide these things or ignore them. You must overlook them each time they occur. But you know that you don't always do this.

Sometimes you do see. And when you do, you can feel your heart swelling. You can feel your heart expanding. How does that feel? When the heart seems to grow, to expand in your chest, sometimes it's so much that you don't know if your body can hold it. Don't worry. It cannot. The body too is an illusion the way you see it. It too is nothing more than love. And when you see this, you will no longer suffer from disease or illness. And if illness should occur it will be a very rare occurrence, and only because you have forgotten who you are for a moment. The illness will then come, simply as a reminder to return to who you are, to return to love. So in this way, even illness is nothing more than love. Love is all you need, as the Beatles sang. And this is true for you. How wonderful. Love is all there is. So when you see this, you will be truly happy. When you see this, your relationships will flower and blossom.

CHAPTER SEVENTEEN

Falling in Love with Love Part Two

THERE IS A BEAUTIFUL SCENE in the movie *Adaptation* starring Nicholas Cage. He plays twin brothers, Charlie and Donald Kaufman. Charlie is a successful Hollywood screenwriter who wrote the screenplay for the movie "Being John Malkovich." Donald is his happy-go-lucky brother who idolizes him, but who seems oblivious to the difficulties and challenges of life around him. Charlie thinks of Donald as naive and an embarrassment.

In the scene I love, Charlie tells Donald the first time he saw him as oblivious to the harsh realities of life. It was in junior high school. Charlie was watching Donald talk to this girl he clearly had a huge crush on. As soon as Donald left, this girl began laughing with her friends about what a loser Donald was. Charlie says, "You were completely oblivious to this and how this girl felt about you." Donald replies, "Oh no. I heard everything she said. I knew how she felt. But I loved her. And that love is my love. Nobody, not even her, could take that love away from me. I can love whoever I want." Instantly Donald went from being the naive, idiot brother, to the only brother who really understood what life and love truly are.

Love is not something out there. It is not something you

need to get from another person. It is not something you are missing until the right one comes along. Love is who and what you are. You are not other than love. Most of us spend our lives not realizing this. And we spend most of our lives searching for it. And it is good to search for this. It is good to search for what we really are. This is the primary motivation of our entire life, whether we acknowledge it or not. And this is just as it should be.

We have these brief encounters when we meet the one. We fall in love. We experience bliss, peace and such powerful love it fills the entire universe. Everything we see is love. This is wonderful, isn't it? In these encounters, we are experiencing who we really are. You can call it love. You can call it the Self or God or Aware Presence. It doesn't really matter what you call it. Words and names are just thoughts. And what you are is not a thought.

Because we are not aware that this experience is actually what we are and have always been, we imagine that it is the other person who created this feeling in us. And without the other person, this whole experience of bliss, peace and love such as the world has never known will be gone. When we imagine it strongly enough, it appears to be real. And so we stop experiencing the bliss, peace and love of our True Self. We stop experiencing ourselves as love. Nothing has really changed except our thoughts. And our thoughts appear real.

Before we met the one, we were love. When we meet the one, we are still love, but now we are aware of what that feels like. We experience it, even though we are not aware of the true Source of this love. After the one has left us or we've left them (it happens), we are still love, but now we are no longer aware of it. The joy, peace and love seem to have left us because we confused the experience of love, the experience of Oneness, as something outside of us and separate from us.

In our experience, sometimes we have love, sometimes we don't. This also happens when a loved one dies. We feel that some part of ourselves has died. We believe that love is outside us in our Beloved. We have not realized that we are love. And so is our Beloved. And so is everything we have ever seen or experienced.

When I was sixteen years old, totally in love, somehow I had the experience that this love I felt was inside me and had always been here. Not only that it was everywhere. Certainly in my Beloved, but also in the air, trees, birds, strangers smiling at me. There was nowhere love was not. I had not been aware of it before I met this particular girl. It was not in her. She was a trigger that awakened this awareness in me. And when I was aware of this, somehow she and everyone else, even complete strangers, loved me. It was like a form of magic. It didn't mean I loved her any less. In fact, I loved her even more. But I knew that the source of this love was not outside me.

I think that was the first time I fell in love with love. That's another way of saying I encountered my True Self as love.

I can't say how often I forgot this as the years went by. Let's just say a lot. But, no matter how stubborn my ego-thought of separation was (world-class stubborn), life helped me remember, again and again through many beautiful beings of love, manifesting in my life like angels. Lovers are always loved. If you feel you're not getting enough love, love more. Love everything and everyone. That's the solution to that imagined problem. And broken hearts happen, but only when we confuse the source of love. And, like all of us, I had a lot of experience doing just that.

The path to awakening through love is not something I have really read or heard about, certainly not in this way, falling in love with love, allowing love to dissolve all imagined separation. It is not the love of an other, even God. It is falling in love with love itself. And this is really what God is. And this is really what you are. And there really has never been any separation at all. We use the names God, I, Self, love, bliss, peace, presence, awareness, and more. But these are all the same thing. There is absolutely no separation. Love can show us this.

In what some will feel is a more practical application, this practice also erases and heals all relationship problems, completely heals loneliness, heals all past relationships still being carried. It eliminates suffering. So it has some practical benefits beyond simply awakening to your True, Unlimited, Infinite Self, although that truly is the end of any problem you could ever imagine having.

I am very grateful for this. It took me a while to really catch on and fully realize and embody this teaching that life has presented to me from birth. I'm a slow learner. But also all the experiences of struggle in between give me real-world experiences to teach from. Thank you for every broken heart. Nothing is wasted.

CHAPTER EIGHTEEN

The Eyes of Love

WHAT DOES IT MEAN to see with the Eyes of Love? You might also ask, what does it mean to see with the Eyes of God – for it is the same thing. How can I tell you how to do this, My Precious One, whom I love more than life itself?

Listen to my heart. Feel my love flowing to you. Feel my love surrounding you and within you. This is God's love, as if you have not already guessed. And you are never absent from God's love. This is the only real thing you can ever rely on. It is pure and constant and infinite and eternal. There is nowhere where there is not God's Love. And so you are experiencing it right now. But to be aware of it, you must open to it. Allow yourself to feel, really feel it. Feel God's love and stop resisting it.

For you see, you must resist God's love in order not to feel it. This is how this world of yours works. You long for God's love; you long to experience who you truly are – which is none other than love. And you long for it because you also resist it. It is ever present and yet you cannot feel it and you look for it and long for it. But here it is, always eternal and infinite. It is actually impossible to escape from it. You can only do that by resisting it with your mind and pretending that it does not exist or that it is not here eternally with you at all times. You must resist this and imagine a world that is filled with death and destruction, separation, isolation and absence from love or only love in special conditions and special relationships. Instead, there is really nothing but love everywhere. It is carried on the air.

It is in the breeze, rustling the leaves of every tree. It is in every bird song. It is in the spider's web. It is in the smile of a child. It is in the touch of a friend's hand on your shoulder when you're sad. It is everywhere. Yet you do not see. It is in the help of a stranger's hand. It is in a kind word. This is where love is. It is in the heroic acts of those who are compelled to act in a natural disaster. It is the comfort of a counselor, fireman or policeman when tragedy strikes suddenly. It is everywhere you look. Even in the greatest tragedy, mostly what there is is love. In fact, that is really all there ever is.

So please learn to look with eyes of love, learn to see with eyes of God. For this is all God sees. And so this is really all that you should see if you want to see Truth. If you want to see what is really here, then you must look with eyes of love.

And yet often we close our eyes to this love, and prefer to hear about the suffering on the news or in the newspaper. We become obsessed with everything that is not love and think about it, worry about it and fret about it – ignoring the truth of love that is everywhere. And this is what we call our life. So we imagine that we live in a dangerous world filled with suffering and injustice and violence. And we believe this is the real world. And we are not happy. We search for happiness but never find it on a consistent basis. Everything that promises happiness, eventually fails to deliver on its promise. This is our world. Or so we think.

But is it? I see a very different world. And you can see this world too. All I see is love. Everywhere there is only love. This is called seeing with the eyes of love. This is also called being awake. This is called waking up the Real World.

CHAPTER NINETEEN

To Know Thyself Is to Love Thyself

YOU ARE PURE, undivided and infinite love, peace and bliss, just waiting to be realized as you.

This infinite Self, taking the form of a human body, appears to be quite limited, vulnerable and separate from others and the world. This is the process of individualization. It is a good and necessary process. And this human body/mind/ego is the pinnacle of individualization. Think of it as a beautiful rose. Each individual rose looks different from every other rose. And this individualization is very beautiful. It is a miraculous process that begins with one undivided, seamless, gapless whole and out of this appears an infinite variety. And our human minds are the tools that create the ultimate pinnacle in this individualization. We do this through the mind's creation of separate names and forms.

Having completed this process of individualization and separation so perfectly, and having lived in this self-created world of separation for so long, there is a longing to return Home. This longing is felt in your heart. As you answer this call, your heart expands. There is a movement toward wholeness. You experience less of this separation and individualization which has up until now been experienced as your life. You experience more expansion, more connection, more wholeness, more peace, more joy and more love.

Before there was a human body, there was no form. There was expansive light, peace, bliss and infinite love. There was no location in space or time. These are human creations. There were no borders or boundaries separating one thing from another. These are also human creations. The purpose of the human body is to experience the very pinnacle of individualization and separation. And then, while still in the body, to experience the freedom, peace, bliss and love, the Divine light that is our True Nature, before we came to identify with the body as our self. While still in the human body, we remember who we truly are. This happens automatically when physical death removes the appearance of separation and individualization. Our purpose in this physical realm is to remember who we are beyond the limitations of the physical realm.

This is what it means to "Know Thyself," as Socrates encouraged his students to do. It is at the same time the only way to truly "Love Thyself." You cannot truly love yourself if you do not know who you truly are. You would only be loving an imaginary creation. Knowing yourself and loving yourself are one and the same.

If the only self you know is a mind-created, limited, vulnerable body/mind separated from the world by the borders of the physical body, then you do not really know who you are. And it is impossible to love this mind-created self, as it is constantly changing. It has no permanent identity. You attempt to create a consistent continuity for it to give it a sense of permanence and solidity. But this cannot be done. Even the body you identify with so strongly is constantly changing. If this is the self you attempt to know and love, you will always be frustrated because it is impossible. You cannot know or love what does not really exist, except in imagination.

You will spend time and effort attempting to know and love this transient, illusory, mind-created self. You will read books about how to love yourself. You will practice different ways of loving, forgiving and improving yourself. This is not a complete waste of time. You are always learning from everything you do.

But perhaps the most important lesson is always the frustration and suffering you experience from your identification with this particular limited, separate self.

You cannot know your True Self, who you truly are, with the mind alone. Your connection with and knowing of your True Self comes through the heart. It is a feeling, not a thought. This feeling is love. Love dissolves the walls of separation and illusion that created the limited sense of a personal self. You do not create the True Self. It is always here. It can neither be created nor destroyed. It has no beginning or end. It takes no effort to be your True Self. It is the absence of effort. It takes great effort to be the self-created, imagined, limited, mind/body self. You must constantly re-create this self. The True Self takes no effort at all. It is always here.

It takes no effort to love this True Self. To love the mind-created self you must picture different aspects of it, forgive the more unlovable aspects, and transform the more unlovable aspects into more lovable ones. If another unlovable aspect appears, you must work with that. It is continuous work and effort. The True Self is unconditional love ItSelf. It takes no effort to love It because It is love. It is simply love loving love. It is the beingness of love. Another term for love is no separation. Love dissolves the illusion of separation. The feeling of no separation is the feeling of love. They are one and the same.

To Know Thyself is to Love Thyself. They are one and the same. You cannot know your True Self and not love your True Self. This is impossible. And you cannot love your True Self without knowing your True Self. This is also impossible. Knowing your True Self and loving your True Self are one and the same.

> "Understand that you are unlimited spiritual beings waiting to be realized, and that within your self is an incredible intelligence. That intelligence has the abil-

ity to supply you with every good thing. Within you is God Source, the source of every good thing in your world. Be open to those intuitions, guidance, and promptings that come from your own heart, once you really choose to live from your heart each day. Understand that even though you are God/Free Will Beings, the Spiritual Presence within you that expresses through your human hearts has within it an infinite intelligence and omnipotent nature. Try to remember that infinity is your true nature and when you appeal to it, it will come forth."

– Akasha

CHAPTER TWENTY

The Glorious Impossibility of Loving Yourself

I THINK WE'VE ALL HEARD that in order to really love another person and have a successful relationship we have to love ourselves first. And this is true. But what self are we talking about? Try as we might, this personal, individual self can be a very tricky thing to love. We may spend many years in therapy, reading self-help books, going to teachers, healers, workshops and retreats, all to learn how to love ourselves. And after all this time and effort, the question remains, "Do I really love myself?" And if we are honest, the answer can only be, "I'm not sure."

I have a dear friend who is a spiritual teacher. He teaches people to love themselves. Whenever we meet, he asks me, "Do you love yourself?" This is not the easiest question to answer, but I answer it in this way, "No, I do not love myself. But I am totally in love with the Self." That seems to satisfy him.

The self and the Self are different in every way possible. The self is personal. The Self is impersonal. The self is unique, special and separate from all the other selves and from life itself. The Self is not unique, not special and not separate from all that exists. The self changes and lasts no longer than the physical body does. The Self never changes and is eternal. And the last difference is probably the most important. The Self is real. The self is an illusion created entirely out of thoughts.

Because the self is an illusion, it can never really be loved. It is constantly changing, for one thing. Sometimes it is a happy self; sometimes it is a sad or angry self. No matter how many positive affirmations you repeat, there are always the repressed unconscious thoughts that contradict them. "I am wonderful and deserve to be loved" is contradicted and cancelled out by the unconscious thought: "I am unworthy and nobody loves me." No matter how many physical, emotional or spiritual self-improvement exercises you do, you are only improving something that never actually existed. No matter how much effort you put in, and how many self-improvement books, teachers and workshops you rely on, you are still left with an illusion. As the spiritual teacher Adyashanti once said, "You can put pearls on a pig, but you can't stop it from squealing."

Why do I say it is glorious that it is impossible to love this self you believe you are? It is the repeated and failed effort to love yourself that finally motivates you to look beyond this illusory self, the ego, and discover your True Self.

And this is real Self Love. To love the Self takes no effort at all. It is impossible not to love the True Self. You need no affirmations. You don't need to take the True Self to the gym. You don't need to take It to spiritual retreats, workshops or teachers to learn to love It. The True Self is Love Itself. The very recognition of your True Self is the experience of unconditional Love.

So when you stop trying to love yourself, when you stop trying to improve yourself by putting pearls on a pig, when you realize that this self has never been anything real, you discover real Love in the form of your True Self. If it were possible to love this limited personal self, you might never discover what love really is. You might never discover who you really are. The impossibility of loving yourself is one of the most precious and glorious gifts we receive. Yes, there are countless books, teachers and workshops devoted to learning to love yourself. The ego doesn't give up easily. Thank God it can never work. It is as impossible to love an illusion as it is impossible not to love what is True. Fortunately, what is True happens to be You.

CHAPTER TWENTY-ONE

The Game

YOU ARE LOVE. You cannot help it because you are it. You can try from time to time. You can pretend you are not love. You can pretend you are a limited being, surrounded by separate limited beings. This is a game we all play and have been playing for a very long time. In fact, let's take a moment to do a little exercise that might help make this particular game a little more clear and a lot more fun.

The Game

Let's play a game, you and I. I promise it will be a very interesting game. You won't find a better one. Are you up for it? It's a game you are very familiar with already, although maybe not consciously.

It goes like this. I will pretend that I am a separate, limited, individual person living in a human body. I will call this character Peter. And you do the same. You don't have to call your character Peter. Call it whatever you like. It's best to choose a name people know you as.

Are you with me so far? I have been creating this character Peter for quite a few years and I've had a lot of help, a lot of input from teachers, parents, friends, lovers, children, as well as dreams, fantasies, fears and passions. After sixty-five years this character is quite complex and well developed, but still changing all the time. And you've been developing your character for

The Zen of Love

quite some time too. It's a very rich and complex character. And we're both still developing our characters. We're creating, inventing, changing and adding to these characters all the time. That's part of the game, part of the experience and adventure. It's fun, isn't it?

And not only are we developing and creating our own characters, I'm also creating your character from my perspective. And you're creating mine. Your creation of my character may be quite different from my creation of my character. And that's a huge part of the fun. That's where the mischief comes in. But it's also where some real learning takes place.

Still with me? This game may be becoming quite familiar now. We've been playing it all our lives. So we're really, really good at it. Really, really, really good! In fact we have become so good that we have forgotten we're even playing a game. The game itself has become reality to us. Some fun, huh? It's like an actor becoming so involved in his part that he completely forgets he is playing a role. I heard that this happened to the comedian Jonathan Winters once. I also heard he needed to be hospitalized. So it's probably not such a good idea to completely forget you are playing a role.

That's why you and I are going to play this game we have been playing all our lives unconsciously (like Jonathan Winters forgetting he was just playing a role), and now we are going to play it consciously, in full awareness that it is just a game and not reality. And this puts the game on a whole other level. It is much more fun this way. You don't take it so seriously. You actually have infinite choices of what your character can be. And you have infinite choices of what my character can be. You can make you anything. And you can make me anything. You are already doing this, but it's unconscious and you have most likely limited your choices quite severely. You've listened to other people's opinions of you as if they were really true. And even when those people are no longer around, you've carried those ideas and opinions with you. And that isn't so much fun, is it?

So now we're going to play this game consciously. We're going to create whatever we like. And sometimes we'll still create things that we don't seem to like. But now we're aware that we chose that, too. Even what we don't seem to like is important for our learning, and is part of the game. When we're conscious of the game, the learning happens very, very quickly. Lessons that may have taken us years or even lifetimes to learn when we were still unconscious, we now learn in months, weeks and even days. It's a very, very interesting game.

As you play the game consciously you will notice a few things. You will notice that the reality of the game seems to dissolve. Before, you would look at a person and be sure they are exactly the type of person you think they are and they would act in ways that reinforced this. Now you are no longer so sure. As you change your projections of that person, you notice that they seem to change in accordance with your projections. How interesting. The hard edges of the game and of life itself seem to be far more soft and permeable than you ever imagined. This is not only true of others in the game; you also see it in your concept of yourself. As you realize who you thought you were is nothing more than a series of concepts, of inventions and creations, most of them not even originating with you, your sense of self expands greatly. It no longer has hard edges marked by the borders of a body, but seems to be as infinite as space. In the game, you realize that anything you think yourself to be, you are. So you begin to let go of the projections of others that no longer serve you or make you happy. And you create new ones that do. You become free and powerful.

The reality of the game can dissolve completely. In that case there is only Oneness. But there is no longer a game. You can do this if you like. It will happen quite naturally anyway. But not before you are ready for it. So don't worry. You created the game. You won't finish it before you are ready to. Until then, let's play. But let's play consciously. It's much more fun this way.

CHAPTER TWENTY-TWO

The Dream

I CAN'T OFFER YOU TRUTH.
Nobody can.
But I can offer you a much better dream.
A dream that is free of suffering, illness, separation, loneliness, disease, poverty, war, anger, sadness and death.
A dream that is completely saturated and overflowing with love, peace and happiness.
This is a dream I can offer you.
This is a life I can offer you.
For your dream is your life.
It is all you know.
It is all you experience.
It is your reality.

And you have the unlimited power to create the dream you want.
You always have.

Stop listening to those who tell you what Truth is,
what facts are,
what evidence is,
what reality is.
They do not know.
They are merely dreamers too.
Just like you.

Just like me.
They only know what their dream is.
And most don't even know they are dreaming.

You don't have to accept anyone else's dream as your dream.
You can choose whatever dream you want,
whatever life you want,
whatever reality you want.
You are already doing this, just unconsciously.
Now be conscious of this.

It is as easy as changing your mind.
It is simply changing your thoughts.
Thoughts create your dream.
Thoughts create your life.
Thoughts create your reality.

You no longer have to accept the thoughts that others want you to think.
You are free.
You always have been.

It's time to create a new dream,
a new life,
a new reality.

It doesn't have to be mine.
It is your dream.
You create what is best for you.

I can offer suggestions of what has worked for me.
We are all in this together.
Even our dreams are not separate.
But you choose what is best for you.
That way we all benefit.

Discover Your Own Awakened Heart

If you don't know what is best for you,
ask your heart.
It always knows.

CHAPTER TWENTY-THREE

We Are All Dreamers

WE ARE ALL DREAMERS. What we believe is good, solid, reliable, indisputable, factual, scientific reality is really only a dream created entirely with our thoughts. That's it. Just a dream. The more we accept and understand that, the more power we have over the dream, which we usually consider our life.

Our thoughts are very powerful. They create our reality. The orthodox, common, agreed-upon reality is one of separation, fear, vulnerability and limitation. I was at a veterinary clinic this morning and this common, agreed-upon, fear-based reality was extremely obvious. You will find the same at most doctor's offices, clinics or hospitals. In fact, you will find it almost everywhere you go. Read a newspaper or turn on the evening news and there it is. This is the dream of separation, fear, vulnerability and limitation. It is the dream of competition for dwindling resources. It is a dream of lack. For one to win someone else has to lose because there clearly is not enough for everyone.

So this is our common, agreed-upon version of reality. This is the common, status quo dream. If you go to a psychiatrist or psychologist, this is the dream they consider normal. We all have varying degrees, beliefs, approaches and unique perspectives on this dream of separation, fear and limitation. But, overall, this is the dream of most of humanity.

And few of our 7 billion brothers and sisters realize that it is

The Zen of Love

only a dream, only one of infinite ways of seeing so-called "reality." Part of waking up is simply realizing that everything we consider reality is really only a dream. The entire "real" world can be completely changed with the change of a single thought. It is not solid, real, reliable, consistent, unchangeable. None of it is. It is all merely thoughts that we believe in.

Once we wake up to this, we realize that we have more options than we thought. This dream of separation, believed in by all our brothers and sisters, really has not served any of us very well. It is the sole cause of poverty, war, illness, violence, anger, sadness and death. It is the cause of all our suffering. But since it is just a dream, just made of thoughts, we can change it. We can create a new dream. We can clearly see that not only does this dream of separation create suffering, it has very little to do with anything that is closer to a higher truth. It is basically kind of insane. But don't tell this to a psychiatrist. Most of them still believe in this dream, which may explain why they have the highest suicide rate of any profession. How could we really be separate from anything else? It is only our beliefs, reinforced by the beliefs of the common human consciousness, that could believe such an insane thought, something so removed and contrary to a higher, saner, more beneficial, beautiful and loving truth.

In this case, it is only logical to move to a higher, saner, more beneficial, beautiful and loving dream. So we do. We leave behind the dream of separation, and we embrace and live in a new dream. This new dream is no longer based on thoughts of separation, but on a feeling in the heart that knows there is no separation and never has been. The old dream becomes transparent. It is as if we can see right through it. It becomes a ghost dream until it fades away completely, much as what happens when we awaken from a sleeping dream. It is very much like that.

This new dream is not the common, orthodox dream. It is not the status quo. It is an entirely new dream that bears very little similarity to the old dream of separation, fear, lack, limits and competition. This new dream has no space and time, as we previously thought them into existence. Instead it has eternal presence. Instead of separation, fear, lack and limits, this new dream has love. Not the love of the old dream, but an unconditional, supreme, divine love that is what we are.

This new dream will not be discussed in psychiatric conferences or symposia. It will not be voted on by members of Congress, nor featured in Presidential debates. You will not even see one story on it during the entire evening news. What you will see there are only varying aspects of the old dream. All solutions to any problems will only be solutions created in that same dream of separation and limitation. So the solutions can never be complete or whole or even successful. Relative, limited success is all that can be expected or even imagined in the old dream.

The new dream is quite different from this. In the new dream, what we considered miracles (unexplainable happenings) are quite common. They are daily events. After a while we no longer call them miracles. They are simply part of this new dream. They are simply part of life.

If you are a dreamer, just like me, why not dream a dream that is beautiful, effortless, abundant, joyful, peaceful, loving? If you are a dreamer, just like me, just like all of us, why not dream a dream of love?

CHAPTER TWENTY-FOUR

You Can Dream Anything You Want

YOU CAN DREAM ANYTHING YOU WANT. You have that power. There is nothing that can stop you. It is your dream, after all. Your True Being is unlimited, infinite, formless, eternal. It is the very substance and source of love. So why not dream a dream of love?

You can dream anything you want. It has always been our choice what to dream. We have just been convinced otherwise by other dreamers. And we believed them. We thought they knew something we didn't. That somehow the apparent authority of parents, teachers, media and others gave them something we didn't have. Some inside special information we needed.

It was never true. They too were just dreaming. And most of their dreams were the unfortunate, limited, separate dreams of most of human consciousness. And somehow we always knew better, didn't we? Right from our youngest age, something inside us knew better than those dreams we were being taught were real. There was just something that was not quite right about them.

Yet we did as we were told. We accepted. We learned. We fit in. We made the best of the situation. Yet something inside always questioned the validity, the reality, even the sanity of what seemed to be going on around us and what other people believed. Over time, as we grew older, the questioning went deeper. It sank into our unconscious. It was no longer a conscious questioning. We began to accept the commonly held belief in separation, lack, limitation and competition. We learned to make the best of this belief and attain its rewards of limited, relative and transient happiness, love and peace.

Yet deep in our hearts, this longing for something deeper and more real never abated. When the dream of separation became its most disappointing, this longing resurfaced into our consciousness, and we wondered again consciously if this dream reality is really all there is. Just as we did as very young children, before the conditioning became too strong. And if we were very fortunate, we began to see again.

CHAPTER TWENTY-FIVE

The Mystic's Guide to Dating

I THOUGHT THIS TITLE WAS AMUSING, but I am serious. Many people are starving for an intimate relationship. This has never been a problem for me. Although many people have asked me, I didn't honestly have a clue why that is. I figured I was just lucky. But now I think I know. Yes, if you want to cut right to the punchline without hearing the joke, it's love. For me that is always the punchline, the solution to all problems. But I certainly didn't always know this, or know how it affects my life. And I think you deserve a little more explanation than simply, "Love is the answer."

So here is my story – and I believe it will help you.

Love and Physical Beauty

My Dad was an extremely handsome man. I mean movie star handsome. Although he was a totally macho guy, he did model for an early Marlboro campaign, when he was begged repeatedly and offered a great deal of money. And women were crazy about him. It was incredible to witness this. Even when he was in his eighties, the young waitresses at restaurants would be giggling to each other, pointing at him and blushing when he spoke to them. And he was never even flirtatious. It was just this very powerful, magnetic attraction. Mostly he seemed oblivious to it. It was just the way life was for him.

And this was not something I was particularly pleased about. I would bring home girlfriends as a teenager, and the conversation would go something like this:

She: "Is that your Dad?"
Me: "Yes."
She: "Really?"
Me: "Yes, that's my Dad."
She: "Wow. I mean wow."
Me: "Could you stop drooling for a moment. He's fifty years old. You're 14. I'm 14. You're with me. Let's go up to my room."
She: "Yeah, I know. That's right. Of course. But... wow."
Me: "Would you like me to arrange a date?"
She: "No. What are you saying? Would you?"
Me: "That's not going to happen."
She: "No. Of course not. I was just kidding. But... wow."
Me: "Okay, you can stop talking now."

He never paid any attention to it, but my Dad was my competition. And that was clearly some major competition. It was like being an artist and Picasso's son. As long as I wasn't being compared to him, I seemed to have at least a small taste of the same mojo.

So what is this mojo? What is the source of this magnetic attraction? I believe the source of this attraction is just the same for women as it is for men. Anyone would assume from what I wrote that it was of course his incredible handsomeness or, if it was a woman, her physical beauty. And we all assumed this as well. It is quite unusual to see a man over six feet tall with the body of a twenty-year-old athlete and movie star handsomeness, all of which lasted well into his eighties. So of course, that is the secret. And if you don't have that, then you're out of luck. If that were so, why would I even bother writing this? The story continues.

We all believed this was true. He was so handsome that we missed the obvious: what I understand now is the true source of this magnetic attraction, of everyone's magnetic attraction. My Dad was one of the most generous and loving people I have ever met. He loved everyone. He was interested in everyone. He just loved people. And it didn't really matter what they did or who they were. The more flaws and weaknesses they seemed to have, the more he loved them. He couldn't have cared less what he looked like. He wasn't interested in himself. He was interested in them. He was just extremely interested in people. When he looked at them, he really saw them, and he liked what he saw. He liked everyone. Although men (at least most men) didn't swoon in his presence the way women did, everyone loved him. He just really loved people. I believe this was the true source of his magnetism. Yes, it came in a nice-looking package. But there are many beautiful people who do not attract this kind of attention. And there are many people who are not typically beautiful who do.

Physical Beauty

As a society we put an enormous amount of emphasis on physical beauty. So it is natural for us to believe that physical beauty is what attracts us. And it may be what initially attracts our attention, but it is only a very small, and mostly unimportant, part of the story. We've already talked about my Dad's physical beauty. It's time we give the other sex some attention.

I'm an artist, and I have been a lover of physical beauty in all its forms all my life. At one point in my life I was a fashion photographer. Not on the level of an Avedon or Scavullo, but I was quite good. I worked in the studio of a major advertising and fashion photographer in New York. He was very overbearing with the models, and many would come to me for support. I got to know some of the models very well and ended up dating some of them. Society considered these the most physically

The Zen of Love

perfect women in the world. So it is hard to imagine how terribly insecure they all were about their looks. They were obsessed with their physical appearance. This is, after all, how they earned their living, and a very good one at that. They were not only self-obsessed but also extremely self-critical. Inside these beautiful packages there was seething insecurity, and even self-loathing. It was both interesting and surprising, and it was terribly sad.

I think they liked me so much simply because I could see all of them and I still loved them. I was young and insecure myself. Although I didn't have their physical beauty, I could very much identify with the insecurity. And for whatever reason, I loved that too. I saw the whole package and I loved the whole package. That was not only irresistible to them, but it was extremely healing, too. When they were with me, or when I was running the photography session, they seemed to glow with an inner light. They became ten times more beautiful than they were before. An inner beauty was ignited that previously had been absent.

Let's face it: physical beauty is, as they say, only skin deep. People who only have physical beauty are shallow and empty. They are like lifeless mannequins. Physical beauty may attract you initially, like a billboard in Times Square, but as soon as you get up close you quickly see that it is only a lifeless, two-dimensional image. There is no depth to it. No naturalness. No Truth. No love. And so what initially attracted you ends up repelling you. And this is an experience that many of these beautiful models faced, time after time. Their relationships with men were very short, and always ended in suffering, loneliness and bitterness.

And who were the men they dated before me? They were very famous or wealthy, or both, like the photographer I worked for. Powerful men. Or male models who were just as beautiful, shallow and self-obsessed as they were. These are considered the standards in America for male sexual attractiveness. Physical beauty, wealth, fame and power. So why would they want to date me? I had no money. I may have been cute, or "interesting" as one model said, but I was no male model. I wasn't famous. And I had no power at all. I was only a lowly assistant to a famous photographer. And I was barely out of my teens myself. I asked that question of myself, and I asked them too. Neither of us knew the answer back then. I was a rare treat for these women. The other men could lavish expensive gifts on them, and even a certain amount of reflected and media status, simply by being with them. But I gave them something they were not used to getting. I gave them love. I actually cared about them for more than their physical beauty. I saw their vulnerability and insecurity and I loved them anyway. And I gave them something else that I was totally unaware of at the time. I could see who they really were. I could see beyond the physical beauty, beyond the insecurity and self-loathing. I could see their True Infinite Self. And this is what I really loved. And to be seen for who you really are, even if you are consciously unaware of it, is a rare gift indeed. It is irresistible. And now I understand that this is really why they were with me.

As a child, I had quite a bit of experience observing the effects of very beautiful women marrying very wealthy, powerful men. Many of my parents' friends were like that, and I was friends with their children. What I observed was that while the wealthy husband was off working, his wife, in their beautiful vacation home, was sleeping with her younger lover, and then criticizing her husband to her friends, including my mother. It happened in most of the families I saw. All these women were also interested in my Dad, who was not wealthy, but he had the decency to resist, at least as far as I know. I felt a great deal of pity for these poor cuckold husbands. This was the life they had worked so hard for. But what kind of life was that? Your wife despises you and cheats on you behind your back. Your children barely know you. And you're working yourself to an early grave. All I could feel was great sadness for these poor men. And I don't think their wives were any happier. In spite of having a lover, they all seemed very bitter and unhappy. It's the American Dream. Why is it so horrible?

Just as with the other men, even these relationships with me couldn't last for long. Although their True Self was pure and infinite love, their conscious self, who they believed they were, was still very self-centered and narcissistic. Mostly what I felt was compassion for the deep loneliness and insecurity they felt. Many models seemed to be like this. But not all. There was one young woman from Maine who was definitely different. She was as physically beautiful as the rest, but she had not lost the natural beauty that was inside her. She didn't need me to make her glow. She was always glowing. I never dated her, although I wished I had. We did become good friends and it felt wonderful just to be around her. I secretly hoped she would not stay in the industry, as I was afraid it might dehumanize her and strip away that natural inner beauty. I suspected that it might have had that effect on the others. For the models that I dated, it felt more like I was taking care of them emotionally or healing them in some way. And I suppose I was. But that's not something you stay in a relationship over. It's too one-sided. Even if you love unconditionally (which I didn't fully at the time), in a relationship you still eventually expect something back. Otherwise what's the point? And with very self-centered, narcissistic people that's just not going to happen.

This was a great lesson for me in what physical beauty is and isn't. It's a nice advertisement. But then the product actually has to deliver some value.

And then I had another lesson in contrasts. About eight years ago I dated a woman I met on an online dating site called Spiritual Singles. In appearance she was completely unlike the women I was usually attracted to, as close to the opposite, in fact, as it might be possible to be. And yet I was irresistibly drawn to her. I still had a checklist at the time. And on that

Discover Your Own Awakened Heart

checklist was that I would not travel more than thirty minutes from my home. I lived in a major urban city, so this seemed a reasonable request. She lived over one and half hours away in another state. What happened was that she wrote me this email, which I found the most irresistibly compelling email I had ever received. I instantly fell completely in love with her, based on this single email. That single email completely burned up all my checklists.

When we were together for about a week and in this miraculous relationship that seemed nothing short of magic, I told her that it was that incredible email that drew me to her so irresistibly. She said, "Are you sure? I don't remember writing an email like that. Why don't you see if you can find it, and read it again."

So I did. I dug up her email, and I was totally shocked by what I read. It was nothing at all. It simply said something like this, "You look interesting. I'm a year older than you. I hope that doesn't bother you. If you're interested I would like to meet you." That's it. In my mind, it was this incredibly romantic email that reached right into my soul. So what the heck was that all about? I learned there is a lot more to attraction and relationships than anything the human mind can conceive of. It is a lesson in awakening. And my lesson began in earnest with this one.

Lilly was and is an amazing woman, an amazing being. In some ways you might call her a Living Saint. She was a yoga teacher and had her own studio. She had an incredible effect on everyone she met. She was the full embodiment of love in a human form. I think you can understand why life needed me to be with her and learn from her. She taught a very early morning yoga class. Her students would come in sleepy, grouchy, their morning caffeine fix not yet taking effect. Even their posture was sleepy and grouchy and uncomfortable. As soon as Lilly walked into the room, everything changed. It was as if the room had become three times brighter. Each one of her students was bathed in this incredible light and love. The whole room was. And her students were so happy. Lilly was always happy. The love in that room was so palpable you could almost touch it, as if it had become physical. Her students were addicted to her. They needed that love fix every morning far more than they needed coffee. She was a wonderful yoga teacher. Gentle and loving. But the love that simply poured out of her being was the real teaching. It was not what she taught but what she was. Lilly was love. She is love. And this is irresistible.

When I was with Lilly, I was love too. Everyone was. Strangers would stop us on the street and say things like, "I'm sorry. I never do this. But I just have to ask. Who are you people? You just seem to be glowing." We would get this all the time. There's nothing you can really answer to questions like that other than, "Thank you." But it is beyond obvious that this state of pure unconditional love has a profound effect on even complete strangers. They can't help but approach you. They are drawn to you like a magnet. Just as I was to Lilly. Just as everyone is.

Lilly did not have the physical beauty that society puts so much value on. She had something else far more valuable. And that's really what this book, and life, are really about.

My Story

Maybe that's where I come in. I never had my Dad's star-quality good looks. When I was young, girls considered me cute. As I got older, I was considered interesting. Or, "There's just something about you." As a teenager, I first noticed that I could get girls interested in me before they even saw me. I would simply focus my attention on them, without saying a word, and across the school cafeteria they would look up and try to find what was making them feel like that. What was making them suddenly feel so good. Or they would turn around in a line when I was standing behind them. Eventually our eyes would meet, and then it would begin. This may sound like an unusual way to meet members of the opposite sex (or same sex if that's your preference). But I don't think it is. I think many people do this without even being aware of it. I just became aware of it at a young age.

It simply took focusing my attention on this one person to the exclusion of everything else in the world, including myself. It wasn't staring. I didn't even have to look at them. I simply focused my awareness – and as I later understood, love – on this one person. And this awoke something in them that they liked very much. And then they liked me. Their mind would tell them it was because I was cute. But the truth is that never had anything to do with it. It still happens today. And women think it is because I have a nice body or a nice smile or kind eyes or that I am sexy. And I used to believe that too. But now I know it is none of those things. Those are merely excuses to be closer to love. Because what women really feel around me is love. Just like they felt around my Dad. Just like I felt around Lilly.

My Dad spent most of his time out in nature. He was very connected to the natural world. He said nature was his church, his therapist and his teacher. And it really was. Spending most of his time in nature, he became natural. He felt the Oneness, the Unity of life. He would never say this. He didn't think in this way. But it was true. Nature does not lie. It only presents truth. If we spend enough time in nature, some of this truth cannot help but rub off on us. It very much did so on my Dad. And I think that this naturalness (very unusual for a human), this sense of connection with life, was always the true source of his magnetism. Women were drawn irresistibly to this like moths to a flame. It was nothing he did, or really even how he looked. He made no effort to create this attraction. He never even thought about it. It was simply who he was. It was his very being. And this very being was the real source of his amazing attraction.

This is what I think of as Being Love. Not loving. Not being loved. But Being Love. And I believe this is the real source of all human attraction. It always seems to have worked for me.

Like my Dad, I don't try to do this. I'm not even sure how you would try. But, unlike my Dad, I am very aware of it. It is very clear that when I am aware of myself as love, a type of magnetic attraction spreads out around me. Again, it is nothing that I do. I just notice it happening.

As a person, we are limited, vulnerable and needy. A person needs many things and worries a great deal about getting them. A person feels that they need love. A person is not aware that they ARE love itself, nor that they are not actually a person at all. So a person has a great deal of trouble dating and attracting people. If you are a person seeking love, then what you are telling other people is that you don't have love and you want to get it from them. And these other people also don't realize they are love. They also feel they only have a limited supply of love or none at all. So with all these people without love, who are searching for love, is it any wonder that so few are finding it? Everyone is worried that the next person might take the little love they have left, leaving them broken-hearted again. It is the dilemma of the person.

But what if you are not a limited person at all? What if you ARE actually the same love that you are seeking? What if you ARE unlimited, infinite and eternal love? Trust me when I say this: if this is what you feel, you will attract people like moths to a thousand-watt floodlight.

Everyone is attracted to love. They make excuses about why they are attracted to a person who is manifesting love. There has to be a logical reason for this attraction. So they will project many ideas on you. It's all quite flattering. But the truth is that none of this is true. Love attracts love. The need for love does not attract love. It attracts need or it simply repels, which is more common. Either way, the outcome is not very good. Since love attracts love, when you are manifesting love this is what you receive – from everywhere. Although I was totally unaware of it then, this is what was happening to me back in high school. This attention I was focusing on girls I was drawn to was simply a very watered-down version of love. But even a watered-down, limited version of love has magnetic power.

When I was young, and sometimes not so young, I thought I was interested in sex. (Possibly obsessed or addicted might be a little more honest.) But I realize now that this too was never true. I was only interested in love. Some of the forms love takes are physical. This is certainly true. And how wonderful that is! But it really is all about love, in whatever manifestation that takes.

When you manifest love, it awakens love in all the people around you. Everyone loves you. It cannot be helped. Most people cannot resist it. There are some very few people who are so disconnected from love that they can come to resent or fear this feeling you have awakened in them. But fortunately for them, and for you, this is quite rare. Love has a very positive magnetic attraction in most humans.

As I said in the beginning, the sole secret to the Mystic's Guide To Dating is love. Not searching for it, or trying to give it to someone else, but being love, manifesting love. When you are love, there is no effort involved. Zero effort. You simply ARE love. You are not doing love. You are simply being what you are. And that is all that needs to happen. We are so used to imagining that success in life takes effort. And we think this is true for dating and attracting relationships too. But the real secret is that it is not, not at all. It is completely effortless. You already are love. We all are this. We are nothing but this. When you do not realize this, you will continue searching and continue being frustrated. So I am simply suggesting that we turn around 180 degrees. Look at what is searching. And see if what is behind this limited person who is searching is none other than the unlimited, unconditional love that you are searching for.

The Zen of Love

When you find this, your dating problems are over.

CHAPTER TWENTY-SIX

Real Love Is Unconditional

ONE OTHER THING I should mention about this love that I am talking about – this love that you are – is that it is unconditional: completely, one hundred percent unconditional. It has no agenda. It has no needs. It has no preferences or judgments. It is completely unconditional. It is simply love being love. And what does love do? Love loves. That's all it does. It doesn't choose to love one person more than another. It doesn't choose not to love someone because they hurt you, abused you, stole your car or broke your heart. It loves anyway. That's all it can do. And it cannot not do this. It is very important to understand this.

The Checklist

I hear many people talking about the type of person they want to be in a relationship with. They have a checklist. They should be spiritually aware or at least open. They should be financially stable. They should be easy to get along with. They should be healthy and physically fit. They should eat or should not eat certain foods. They should have similar interests. You know what I'm talking about. You probably have your own checklist. I know I had mine. And you know what happened to my checklist. Each time, life blew it right out of the water. If I wanted A, life gave me B. If I wanted B, life gave me C. Life never cooperated with my checklist. And after some time feeling frustrated, I realized that life was totally right and my checklist was totally wrong. I see that many people have not learned this valuable lesson yet. So let me say it again. I learned that my checklist was totally wrong and life was totally right. Any checklist is just your mind making more lists, creating more preferences. And you know what? None of it has anything to do with life as it really is. They're just fantasies. Pure imagination. Disney movies. Life always knows exactly what you need. Get used to it. It's always been like that and it always will be. And thank God for that.

Sure, life may present you with some pain. But that's just to help you wake up from the conditioned dream world most of humanity lives in. Yes, it's painful. Nobody likes a broken heart. Nobody likes pain. But each broken heart has a purpose. Its purpose is to get you to look deeply into yourself and find this love that I'm talking about. And isn't that worth a dozen broken hearts?

So I threw my checklist right out the window. I see many things that have never been on my checklist, or anyone's checklist. And I love them anyway. That's all love can do. Love loves. And I learn so much from each of those things that were never on my checklist. They are invaluable to me. Because it is those things that would never be on my checklist or anyone's checklist that have brought me Home to my True Self as Love.

The truth is that if I ever found anyone who satisfied everything on my checklist, I would have a very boring, predictable life. I would never grow. I would remain stuck in my little checklist dream world. So I am so grateful that this has never happened. And maybe, if you think about it, you are too. You might want to join me in throwing your checklist out the window, and allowing life to show you its true miracles. It's just waiting to do this, you know. It only needs your willingness and attention.

CHAPTER TWENTY-SEVEN

Sex and the Spiritual Path

ANY BOOK MUST BE MADE OF STORIES. And all stories must be of the dream. Truth has no stories. It is entirely complete in and of itself. From the perspective of Truth, there is no need for this book, or anything at all. It is already one hundred percent complete.

But still this book has emerged. Although not Truth Itself, it points back to the Truth from which all things arise. The stories in this book touch people and evoke some sense of what is beyond the dream. Writing it has also been an important process for me. There is a need to be completely honest, completely vulnerable and completely naked. This not only touches a universal chord in others, but it allows me to be honest with myself in ways I may not have done without this deep introspection and unraveling.

The issue of sex and spirituality has been a major one for me. There has been a powerful inner struggle for much of my life. One side pulls me toward monkhood, and the other toward the very intense and sometimes overwhelming passions that have always seemed to be an essential component of my life.

Since my first girlfriend at age five, I have always loved women. And this love only increased as I grew older. It grew into an intense and frequently overwhelming passion. I will be nakedly honest here. I love the feel and scent of a woman's hair, the touch, smell and glow of her skin, her neck, her ears, her nose, the softness of her mouth, the infinite depth of her eyes, the feel and rhythm of her breath and heartbeat, her breasts, the arch of her back, the swell of her hips, her arms and incredible fingers, her legs and toes, and the yielding, inviting, hunger and fulfillment of her womanhood. I think you get the point. There is not a single millimeter of a woman's body that I am not totally and utterly in love with.

But it's not just the body I fall in love with, not by any means. It's the complete package. It's the hidden vulnerability and fragility, and the powerful inner strength and incredible, bottomless, inner resources. It's the caring, compassion and love. It's the undying friendship and fierce loyalty. It has only been women that I could ever share my deepest secrets with, the things I was afraid to admit even to myself. Instead of being repelled or criticized, my tears were always met with the care, compassion and love of the mother I never had.

There's something even more important. And this is where sex truly merges with spirituality. This in the end is the true reason for my overwhelming passion. It is the merging into Oneness, two apparently separate beings becoming One. It is the gazing into another's eyes until there is no longer a seer and one who is seen. It is the physical joining that turns both bodies into one body and then dissolves even that one body. In this way, sex and love emerge into Truth. They have always pointed to this. The intense passion for the body and the person are all signposts pointing to this merging, this Oneness, this Truth.

But this does not happen with just any woman. I can only be with one particular woman at a time. And this woman is in some way chosen for me. I can't explain this adequately – even to myself. But somehow the perfect woman always shows up, exactly who is needed, at exactly the right time. As I said, I can't explain this, but it has never once failed to happen. And when it does, I can do nothing but surrender completely and utterly.

In the past I tried to make choices, make decisions, use some logic. I had checklists for the type of woman I was looking for. But this turns out to be pointless. It is nothing but an arrogant joke that I could make a better decision than life does. Eight years ago I finally stopped doing this, and now I simply go along for the ride.

To learn the lessons that any relationship brings takes a certain amount of time. And it also takes time to explore a woman thoroughly, to become truly intimate. It is also why I don't particularly like traveling. I like to stay in one location and become thoroughly intimate with it. And that takes time, just as it does with a woman.

For whatever reason, unlike my male friends, I was never focused on receiving my pleasure from a woman. That always came without my seeking it. But somehow, her pleasure IS my pleasure. It has always been like this. And unlike complaints I have heard about being bored with their sexual partner, I have never experienced that. I was married for twenty years, and sex only became increasingly more intense, passionate, intimate and interesting each year. As I said, it takes time to really explore intimately, and the depth of this exploration and intimacy appears infinite.

At some point it became very clear that sex was not about sex; it was about love. When love was not involved, it was shallow and somehow incomplete. It was like a tiny fraction of sex, valueless and meaningless. I often found myself, against my will, falling in love with women I had just met and fallen into bed with. Try as I sometimes did as a young man, I could not help falling in love with any woman I became sexually intimate with. This was not what the sexual revolution of the sixties, the hippies and groupies, was supposed to be about. There were times when I felt there was something wrong with me. But really it was just the opposite.

Love is really about Oneness, about the end of the illusion of separation. Of course, relationships are not necessary for this. Because of this inner struggle between the monk and the lover,

I embarked on some extended experiments with celibacy, something I had rarely experienced since before I was fourteen. Three times I went for almost a year before beginning a new relationship. This was very new for me. In the past, as soon as a relationship ended, I was looking for the next one. And it always seemed to be there, as if just waiting for me. Three weeks was about the longest time I had ever spent between relationships. And even that seemed very long for me.

So these extended periods of celibacy were very new for me – and, much to my surprise, incredibly rewarding. Strangely, I felt even closer to this Oneness and non-separation than I did in relationships. Even now I'm not exactly sure why. Since I didn't have the emotional or physical demands of a relationship, I spent more time meditating and doing other spiritual practices. For the most part, I was on an extended retreat, and I limited my contact with people during these times. It just seemed natural to do this. There wasn't really a plan. It just happened, along with the decision not to seek another relationship.

And in this time of silence and solitude, many things blossomed inside. One of them was this great sense of Oneness and connection to all of life. Instead of feeling lonely, I felt completely full and connected. I never actually felt less alone than I did during those times when I was technically alone. So the monk side of me seems to be just as natural as the lover.

While I was in solitude and being celibate, in my monk lifestyle, I had no desire, or even a thought, of being in an intimate relationship again. It seemed clear that part of my life, which had been so much of my life, was now over. And then, quite suddenly, it wasn't over. Each time I would find myself feeling as though it was time to emerge from my cave, like a hibernating bear feeling the coming rush of Spring. It's not that I was hibernating or waiting during those periods of isolation. I was learning and transforming and flowering every day. But there was a sudden shift. Life was clearly saying, "Now it's time for something new."

The moment I emerged from the cave of solitude, there was the relationship just waiting for me, along with its lessons. And I need to point out the importance of the lessons. All relationships, I have learned, are principally about the lessons they teach. That's what their real purpose is. It's much easier if you understand this now. They're not about the relationship themselves, "till death do us part," "put the relationship first," "soul mates," "twin flames," that kind of thing. Those are very romantic ideas, and they have their place. But they are ideas. Relationships, and life itself, are about learning what we need to learn. That is really, and only, what they're for. It's very important to know this.

The passion, the desire, the yearning, the longing, the devotion, even the love are only means to get us into the relationship so we'll learn what we're supposed to learn. Get it? That's all it's ever about. When you realize this, you will throw away your checklist and your preferences and enter the relationship presented to you willingly and completely, because this is the most effective way to learn. And this is also why we don't want to have multiple partners, although that too can be a useful lesson early on because it usually leads to suffering pretty quickly. But the main lesson here is: simply don't do it. It takes time to learn the lesson completely. And there is one perfect person to learn that particular lesson with. And that person is always the very same person you happen to be with. Surprise! Life never makes mistakes. Trust what life brings. When the lesson is over, so is the relationship.

If you're a very slow learner, or have multiple lessons to learn from the same person, the relationship can last for twenty years or a lifetime. If it's only one lesson and you're a quick learner, which means you accept, understand and absorb the lesson fully, the relationship may only last for a month or so. It's all perfect. The one thing you don't want to do is stay in a relationship after the lesson has been learned. That's a big mistake. We often call these loveless marriages. They're tragic and pointless. "Staying together for the kids" just creates suffering for you and the kids. Please move on to the next lesson. That's what life is about. In our hearts we always know when the lesson and relationship are over. We don't need counseling. We need to move on.

In our culture we don't understand this. We need people to stay in marriages and relationships as a form of social control. The result is too often misery and suffering. It's possible that an old relationship could have new lessons to teach. But that means the old relationship must also change, grow and evolve, and so must each of the people involved in it. And still there's no guarantee this will work. Only life itself knows which people are best for the particular lessons that must be learned. We have no control over this. We have our wishes, desires and preferences, but we really have no control. Life knows. We don't. We are the students and life is the teacher. It's not the other way around.

CHAPTER TWENTY-EIGHT

Invaluable Lessons of Heartbreak

HEARTBREAK IS SOMETHING MOST OF US FEAR. And after experiencing heartbreak a few times, we can become more reluctant to give ourselves fully in a relationship. This is tragic. At least some part of every relationship is about heartbreak. It is very painful, but also an important part of learning to love and learning who we really are.

It might sound absurd to say this, but I will anyway because it's so important. Welcome the heartbreak. Your most important lessons will usually be wrapped in the wrapping paper of heartbreak. Do not run away from it. Open the package. Find out what's inside. Here is one of your greatest lessons from your entire relationship.

I will tell you about some of the great transformative lessons I have learned from heartbreak. I have already told you about my first girlfriend, Ginny, when I was five years old, and how I broke both her heart and mine simultaneously when I was six. From this heartbreak I learned that to break another's heart is to break your own. The belief that there ever were two separate hearts was just illusion. Ginny was me and I was Ginny. To break her heart, my own heart had to be broken also. I think you can admit this was quite a profound realization for a six-year-old. Do you think there is any other way possible for this profound lesson to be learned? I can't imagine what it would be.

The Zen of Love

Since I am being nakedly honest, here is a more recent story. Not long ago, life led to me to a relationship with a woman I will not name here, for her sake. Beware of getting involved with writers who are nakedly honest, or spiritual teachers who teach with their life. I don't keep anything secret. Nothing is personal to me. Everything that happens in my life can and will be used for your benefit, My Beloved Reader.

I learned many things from this woman. All relationships teach. And many of these lessons were wonderful. I learned how to listen to and understand the natural world, and realize that I was not separate from it. I learned to surrender more fully. All of these were painless and enjoyable lessons. But the biggest and most profound lesson came through very intense heartbreak. And she was the perfect person to create this particular learning experience. Nobody else I had ever been with would do what she did on that one particular night.

We lived in a three-story house, with porches on the two upper levels. In the summer we left all the windows and porch doors open at night to cool the house down. She informed me that a friend was going to be visiting us for a few days while he attended a tantric conference nearby. She introduced me to him. He seemed like a very nice fellow. He slept on an air mattress the first night, on the upper deck porch. My office was just below the upper deck. You could hear everything on the porch through the open windows and doors. The first night I just heard his snoring. That didn't bother me. The next night while I was writing some Facebook posts, I heard something else.

You might know that an air mattress can be very noisy if you're moving on it in a certain way. And she and her friend were. They were having sex outside on the porch. It was not long, but it was very loud. I could hear everything. My stomach dropped to the floor. I couldn't believe it. She was a tantric teacher, but we had agreed over a year earlier that if we began a relationship, we would be sexually exclusive. It was the way I had always done it from the time I was a teenager. Too many bonds are created in sexual intimacy to bring others into it. It creates a disturbing energy, at least to someone as empathic and connected as I am.

At the time I was already a spiritual teacher. I lived a calm life of peace, love and bliss, maybe not as much as I do now, but it was coming close. In that instant all calm was gone. My peaceful center was shattered. I felt intense inner turmoil. It was so intense that I knew it was triggering more than just the disturbing event happening just outside my window.

Although the event itself did not last long, what was triggered lasted for days. I felt deeply the initial abandonment I had experienced in the womb from a mother who did not want to have a baby. And later, when she left two days after my birth, and I didn't see her again until I was three months old. I experienced this initial experience of abandonment – and many subsequent ones – fully and intensely, right up to the one happening outside my window. As I followed this chain of perceived and experienced abandonments, I felt each one more intensely than the one before.

It was intensely painful and intensely revealing. I couldn't sleep at all for two days. The next morning I asked her to leave and stay at a motel. She refused, and she actually seemed happy that I was so upset. It had bothered her that try as she might, she hadn't been able to trigger me into anger or sadness. And finally she had. It was proof of her ability to bring a spiritual teacher "down to Earth"; down to suffering. She had certainly succeeded.

Seeing that I was so upset, a friend who was leaving for Washington for a few weeks gave me the keys to his house. I cried for two days straight, hardly sleeping at all. It was not only for my heartbreak over this imagined betrayal and abandonment; I was crying for every event of abandonment I had experienced throughout my life. And there seemed to be a lot of them. Most of these I had repressed deep in my subconscious, especially those I'd experienced in infancy. But now they were all coming up to be re-experienced and re-lived. This one action had triggered a flood of repressed feelings.

At this moment you may be thinking about what value all this suffering could possibly bring. Stay with me and you'll see. On the third day, a deep revelation hit me with the force of a nuclear explosion. And this revelation could not have happened in any other way. The severe pain of this suffering opened a door that could not have been opened any other way. It cracked the wall for me of whatever ego still remained. And through this crack, I could see clearly that the separate person I thought I was had never existed. If I had never existed as a separate person, then my mother could never have abandoned me at birth. She could go to the other side of the planet and never be an inch separate from me. None of the other abandonment experiences could have happened either. And my girlfriend and her friend were also not the slightest bit separate from me in any way.

In that moment I clearly knew who I was. I was not separate from anyone or anything. And in that knowing, I also knew my girlfriend, my mother, and everyone else in a way I never had before. I cannot describe what that is in words. It is a feeling, a direct experience as profound as any human can ever experience.

I spent the rest of the day alternately crying and laughing. But now my tears were of the highest gratitude and love. And my laughter was at clearly seeing the enormous absurdity of who I believed I had been. My entire life and everything I had believed were instantly exposed as pure delusion and ignorance. You can do nothing but laugh when you finally see this. I felt like the biggest idiot in the entire world. Everything I had believed about life was based on this single belief that I was a separate person, trying to make my way in a world of separate people. And this had never been true. I was teaching this to others, but I had never really experienced it so fully and completely as I did on that day.

There had never been any separation. There had never been any abandonment. There was never a separate person to be abandoned or to have anything else happen to him, good or bad. It was all a dream.

Life was nothing but a seamless whole, complete and perfect in every possible way. And without this heartbreaking event in my life, I would never have known this in such a deep way. Everything that occurred, only occurred for my benefit. It could be no other way. We often believe we know what is in our best interest. But I can tell you that we don't. We don't have a clue. We don't even know who we are. The truth is that everything that happens is for our benefit. There are no exceptions to this.

My intense pain and anger toward my girlfriend transformed into intense gratitude and love. I knew who I was and I knew who she was, even if she didn't. There was no separation between us. For someone who does not understand what I am talking about, and how can you if you have not experienced this great liberation, what I am going to say next may surprise you. I called her up and showered her with love and gratitude. I saw her as her Divine Self, and I knew, even if she didn't, that everything she did was only for this incredible awakening that I had just experienced. It was the Divine Self serving the Divine Self, and there had never been more than One.

We got back together for a few weeks of love and bliss. It didn't last forever. Does it really need to? The lessons it came to teach had been learned. It served its purpose perfectly. And I'm sure she learned from this as well. It is always like that. Some lessons take a lifetime to learn. Others may be completed in months, weeks or days.

The human mind never seems to understand what lessons are required. And that's a good thing. If it did, it might run from the more painful ones before they were learned. Would I have entered into that relationship if I knew the extreme pain I would suffer before the lesson was learned, even if I knew the glorious results at the end? Probably not. That's the way we are as humans. We seek pleasure and avoid pain at all costs. But often it is the painful lessons that are the greatest teachers. And this is why even heartbreak is entirely for our benefit. If all we want to do with our life is seek pleasure and avoid pain, we're not going to have a very satisfying life. We're not going to grow. We're not going to evolve. We're not going to wake up. And I can tell you now that the bliss of your Awakened Self is worth anything and everything, no matter how painful, that it takes to bring it forth.

CHAPTER TWENTY-NINE

Two Relationships - How and Why We Choose Suffering over Love

I HAVE A FRIEND who came to me for counseling and healing. He had been losing sleep over a decision he just could not make. He was in love with two women, and he could not choose between them. He had been with both women for an equal amount of time. With one woman he felt unconditional love, and she felt this for him. Their relationship was smooth, beautiful and peaceful. They had never had even one fight. He knew she was always there for him no matter what. He felt happy and loved with her. He felt loved not only by her but also by her parents and friends. It was what we might call an ideal relationship. These relationships are great gifts.

The second relationship was a great contrast to the first. He frequently felt rejected and unappreciated by this woman. She often projected her father or other men who had mistreated her onto him. They felt a great deal of passion for each other, but the relationship was tempestuous. My friend described it as being inside a hurricane. There were great highs, but even more lows. Her parents hated him.

Which relationship would you choose? It seems obvious on the surface, doesn't it? But my friend was leaning strongly towards the second relationship, the relationship we would call dysfunctional (or even hellish) and not the first, which we might call ideal. Why would he do this?

There are many reasons people make decisions that are not in their best interest. You would be surprised how many people do this. In *A Course in Miracles*, it says, "We do not know what is in our own best interest." And listening to my friend tell his story, this could not be more clear. The closer he got to making a decision to live with the second woman, the more unhappy and confused he became. But something was driving him to make that decision. What could that be? It was certainly not God or love. There are many things at work here. One is that he did not feel worthy of the love he shared with the first woman. It was too pure. And the relationship was too easy. He didn't have to work at it. As he put it, "It provided no challenges. And I like a challenge." A relationship that works and that is beneficial to both partners does not take work. It is easy. You love each other. What could be simpler than that? But if you feel you have to earn love, if you believe you must work hard to be worthy of receiving love, then a truly loving relationship will not make sense to you.

He grew up in a family where love was not expressed. And this is where he learned what love is. This is very normal in our society. Many if not most families are not grounded in love. Love is there, but it is twisted and distorted. Even the children are taught that they must earn their parents' love with good behavior. Love becomes a competitive act.

And these are some of the reasons why my friend was leaning toward a very dysfunctional relationship, rather than one that promised true happiness. The choice as he described it to me could not have been more clear. And yet he used a variety of rationalizations to justify why the second relationship was the best, and only, choice that he could make.

This is also something many of us do in all aspects of our life. We settle for a job we don't like, rather than take a chance on one we might love. We shy away from trying activities or skills we would love to master, but believe we are not capable of. We settle for a normal, okay life, rather than attempting to soar to heights that we believe are impossible for someone like us.

And in many ways, this is what my friend was doing too. He was presented with the gift of an ideal relationship. It arose easily and effortlessly, a gift of God and love. It was a relationship in which he found peace, love and happiness. And yet he was drawn to a relationship that offered the opposite of this. He was drawn to a relationship that offered suffering. He was drawn to conflict, tumult and strife, just as he had experienced in his childhood home. He had many justifications for this. We all do when we make such choices, which are not in our best interest. And many of these justifications are quite complex and intricate.

Truth, on the other hand, is incredibly simple and obvious. And for many of us that makes it not so interesting. We consciously or unconsciously choose a life of conflict, drama and strife. We choose a life of suffering. It makes no logical sense. But when have humans been logical? We create our own logic to justify our decisions, especially when they run counter to our best interest.

In his heart, my friend knows the truth very well. We all do. The truth is that there is no choice. We do what is in our and everyone else's best interest. And this is usually very clear, just as it is in this case. The confusion between making decisions is because something in us very much wants to make the wrong decision. Something in us very much wants us to suffer. When this leads our life, suffering is what we get. It is never hard to find suffering when you are looking for it. It may seem illogical or even insane when you look at it from this perspective. But this is actually normal behavior for most of us. And this goes a long way toward explaining the high rate of suffering in the western world: the high rates of divorce, depression, alcoholism, drug addiction and suicide. If your goal is to find suffering, you will not be disappointed, just very unhappy.

But this is not the end of the story. There is always the choice of redemption. Suffering itself points you back to the path where suffering no longer exists. We make the conscious or unconscious choice to suffer until we no longer do. And when we no longer do, we are on the path to awakening and love.

CHAPTER THIRTY

The Doorway Home

THE FIRST FEW MOMENTS of a new love are ecstatic. The entire world vanishes, and there is only you and your beloved. And that is more than enough. People remark how your eyes, face and skin seem to glow with an inner light. You look twenty years younger, and you are. Every cell in your body vibrates with this ecstatic aliveness. Your heart is so overflowing with joy that you know life couldn't possibly get better than this.

And you would be wrong.

The moment you first discover your True Self is like this, and amazingly, it is a thousand times more so. It is almost too much for this limited body to stand. But there is a difference. No matter how hard you cling to it, that first ecstatic experience with your beloved tends to change and fade over time. The awareness of your True Self only deepens. As an infinite Self, it has infinite layers to reveal.

That first blush of ecstasy with your beloved is pointing to something. Yes, it's true that it reinforces your ego. "Somebody loves me", says the ego. That's proof that I'm real. If that were so, that ecstatic love would continue growing, instead of fading. But that ecstasy is not without merit or truth. It's pointing to a deeper and truer ecstasy, a peace, love and bliss that has no ending and no beginning. It is pointing to a bliss that continues to deepen throughout endless time. It's no coincidence that the doorway to the Infinite is discovered in the human heart: the Spiritual Heart to be more specific. It's only when we believe that this comes from another person, that this other person is the Source of this ecstatic experience, that we lose our way.

We have always had this. We have always been this. Long before we ever met our beloved, this is what we are. This is our True Self. And this heart that sometimes feels overwhelmed with love, gratitude and bliss is our doorway Home.

CHAPTER THIRTY-ONE

The Dance of Leela

YOU ARE AN EXPRESSION of the Divine Self dancing with Itself. The One Divine Self expresses Itself in many forms. You are an expression of the Self. I am an expression of this same Self. Each of our expressions is unique. And this is just as it should be. It is all part of the perfection of life. The Self dances with and learns from Itself through these expressions. And it dances in many ways. It creates art, paints pictures, makes music. It makes love. It writes things like this. It sees sunsets and gazes into the eyes of Itself in the expression of a Beloved. And yet the Self really only sees Itself because the Self is all that is really ever Here.

Love is really simply the Self seeing and recognizing the Self. When one expression of the Self gazes into the eyes of another expression and sees the same Self, this is love. When we are not yet aware of the Self, we can only imagine it is something else, something far more limited. We might call this the ego.

When we are aware of the Self, we know that we are the Self, and so is everything we see. The Self only sees the Self. The exquisite miracle of life is that the Self expresses Itself in such infinite variety. In India, this is called the Dance of Leela.

Perhaps nothing is more sacred than the conscious act of two humans making love. Two expressions of the same Supreme Self come together as unique individual expressions, one male and one female. They appear to be opposites, yin and yang. They are perfect expressions of the seeming duality that all of life appears as, from entire solar systems to grains of sand. This one man and one woman represent all of this, the sum total of all life. And these two are drawn together by some power that neither truly understands – yet neither can resist. This power is the sacred act of the Self calling the Self back Home to wholeness.

These two expressions of the One Self, believing they are separate individuals, separate from each other and all the world, are pulled toward each other in a magnetic attraction of great passion they cannot resist. And in their coming together, they represent this essential wholeness. The two in this duality become the One of the Supreme Self. You can use the word God for the Self if you like. They are not separate. The joining of this couple in love symbolizes the Eternal Oneness of God. This is the Dance of Leela, the dance of all life, symbolized in this one sacred act between a single man and woman. And it is happening everywhere in life. I use the example of a man and woman only because this has been my experience. The same dance of two becoming one can happen with same-sex couples, or with anyone who experiences this great power that pulls two people together until they become one: this power we know as love.

The Dance of Leela happens everywhere in the universe. It is not only two people making love, but also the gravitational pull of planets circling the sun that creates our solar system, and in the life-giving energy of the sun itself. When a plant stretches its leaves or branches to receive the nourishment of the sun, it too is making love. It too is becoming One. And both the plant and the sun are none other than this very same Self.

If you look with awakened eyes, you too can see this. You are at once the Self that is looking, and the same Supreme Self that is being seen. Everywhere you are only seeing your Self. And everywhere you are the continuous dance of two becoming One, the multitude of infinite variety returning to unity as the One Self. This is the miracle that is taking place everywhere you look.

The dream occurs only because you do not see the Self. You do not recognize or remember who you truly are. You imagine that this expression, unique and beautiful as it is, is all there is of you. You mistake the expression for what you are. In doing this, you have forgotten the Self. It is nothing more than forgetting. Yet life is always showing that you are much more than this. The greatest demonstration of this is love. When two become one, you are pointed back Home to your wholeness. In love, a glimpse of the Self is always seen. In love, you begin to feel whole and complete again. In love, you begin the return Home to the Self that you are, and have always been. And of course this feels wonderful!

CHAPTER THIRTY-TWO

The Purpose of Every Relationship

THE TRUE PURPOSE of every relationship is for your learning. You may think it's because you've finally met Mr. or Ms. Right. You may think it's because you're lonely and you want company. You may think it's because you are horny and want sex. You may think it's because you want children. You may think it's because you want security, to make your parents happy or simply because it's what you're supposed to do. You may think you enter into a relationship for many reasons. But there is really only one reason. You enter into a relationship because it is the best way to learn what you need to learn. Notice I didn't say want to learn. I said NEED to learn.

How do relationships teach you what you need to learn? They teach you through mirroring. You don't yet know who you are. You have forgotten completely. You are firmly convinced you are this separate, unique body/mind walking around, doing things and having experiences. Relationships show you who you really are. They are never about the other person. They're only and utterly about you, but not the you that you think you are.

When your relationship begins, the sparks of love ignite into a full blaze. You have fallen in love and you have fallen hard. You see your Beloved as the most perfect person you ever met. If not perfect for the world, he or she is unquestionably perfect for you. This is your first look at your True Self. When you see your Beloved, it is really the Divine Self winking back at you.

"Hello, My Beloved Self, can you see me now? Let me re-introduce your Self to you. Still can't see me? That's okay. We'll work on it. I'm always here for you because I'm always here as you."

But we don't see this. We believe it's our Beloved soul mate we're seeing. And this is why it's so interesting. This is why we need so many lessons before we finally see. We're still unable to see our True Self, so these mirrors appear in our life until we can.

In the falling-in-love stage, we look at our True Self and it's so wonderful, so beautiful. We're in bliss. We're in love. Life has never been so perfect. And this is also, not surprisingly, what the True Self is. The experience of remembering our True Self is much like the experience of falling in love. We are in bliss. We are in love. Life is perfect. As the wonderful spiritual teacher Mooji often says, "Same, same." The experience of falling in love and the experience of the True Self are not exactly the same, but they're close enough for you to realize that you have experienced something very close to awakening in your ordinary life if you have ever fallen in love.

So what happens after the falling-in-love stage, when things often don't appear quite as rosy? It's still a mirror, but it's reflecting something different. When you were so deeply in love, the mirror reflected your True Self, or as much of it as you could handle at the time. At some point, your ego re-emerged and distracted you from seeing your True Self. Now you're seeing your ego. It's a very different kettle of fish. This is going to be hard for your ego to accept. The ego's job is to project itself out onto the world so you won't notice what it's doing to you. You're still not seeing your partner. And instead of seeing glimpses of your True Self, you're seeing your own ego. And this is also a wonderful lesson. As long as your ego is running the show, you will not remember your True Self. You will be trapped in this dream of separation that you still imagine is real life.

Let's look at some examples of how this works. We'll start with a big one. "What if my husband is physically abusing me? That can't possibly be me. I didn't give myself these black eyes." These types of relationships are tragic. They are brutal. And we often wonder why anyone would stay in a relationship like this. And here's why they do.

It may seem very clear that the husband is the victimizer and the wife is clearly the victim. And on face value this is true. But when we understand the mirror principle we have to look a little deeper. There are many reasons wives stay in these abusive relationships. And they all have to do with what she's telling herself about herself. And she's often not even aware of this.

"I deserved it." "I'm so terrible that if I ever left him I could never find another man. Who could ever want me? I'm lucky to even have him." "Next time I'll be a better wife and maybe he won't beat me." "I'm not good enough." "No one could ever love me."

Her husband may abuse her once a week. But she's abusing herself every day. She's abusing herself twenty-four hours a day. She's even abusing herself when she sleeps. Her husband is mirroring her ego, her false thoughts and beliefs about who she is. Her ego covers up her true beauty and perfection as her True Self by presenting this terribly distorted picture. Her husband may physically abuse her on the outside, but she's abusing herself far more brutally and consistently on the inside. And that's where the real damage is done.

Unless these inner thoughts are corrected, even if she leaves her husband she will quickly find another mirror just like him. Life will always provide the correct mirror. This is why abused women always go from one abusive relationship to another. This sad cycle cannot be broken until the inner abuser is kicked out. Once the inner abuser has been evicted, the mirror will supply a very different reflection. The next relationship can no longer have abuse in it. That lesson was successfully learned and now it's time for a new and hopefully gentler and more loving one. As the ego becomes more and more cleansed, which means less and less prominent in one's life, the lessons become increasingly easier and less painful.

Relationships are only painful because the ego they are reflecting is causing you pain. The purpose of the relationship is to show you what you are unable to see on your own. For some time, you will mistake the reflection for the other person. They are only reflecting you. That's all they can do. If they have negative qualities that are not in you, they won't bother you a bit. You will barely notice them at all. You only see what is in you. That's how mirrors work. Your partner is a perfect mirror for you. If they neglect you, look inside and see how you're doing this to yourself. You're neglecting yourself and looking for someone outside to fill that gap. Nothing outside can fill what you've taken from yourself. When you learn to return to loving yourself, the outer world and all the people in it will reflect that by loving you. This is how these perfect lessons work.

How do I know these things? I can only write about what I have experienced directly. These are not theories, concepts, philosophies or beliefs I have read in a book. If that's all they were, I would probably not believe them myself. I can only express the very deepest Truth of my heart. And you, My Beloved, deserve nothing less.

I have watched this very same process in my own relationships. And, just like you, I was completely unaware of it for a long time. As I became aware of what was happening, often by seeing it in others first, the quality of my relationships began to change. In my current relationship, I mostly just see and experience love, pure innocence and joy. This book itself owes much to this relationship. It would probably not exist without it. The lessons I'm learning are different. Where in the past some things my partner did might have triggered me in some way, now they float through me like air. They have no place to stick. The mirror can only reflect what's in you. If it's not in you, you can't see it. It's invisible. And seeing this is also a great lesson. I see and experience love, because that is what I am. When I see Ahna and experience this great love, I know I'm looking at my Self. I'm no longer fooled. In this case, my Self expresses Itself in a very beautiful form. And this is all entirely for my benefit. This is exactly what I needed.

Not all my relationships and lessons have been so blissful. But none have been anything but perfect. None have been anything but entirely for my benefit. When I had deep unconscious beliefs of unworthiness and abandonment, those beliefs needed to be exposed, shaken loose and finally dissolved through reflections appearing in my life for just that purpose. And even with Ahna, there were still a few hidden beliefs that needed to be burned away in the beginning before the Self could be revealed as clearly as it is now.

In this way, you might say that every relationship is a perfect relationship. Every relationship teaches you what you NEED to learn. As humans, we are the most stubborn beings on this planet. The ego does not let go of its pet beliefs easily. Letting go of these beliefs is dangerous for the ego. Since it is itself only a belief, letting go of beliefs is like committing suicide for the ego. Contrary to the ego's beliefs, you are not the ego but something far greater and more wonderful. So this suicide is not a bad thing. The death of the ego means a return to your True Life. And you've already tasted what that's like when you fell in love.

CHAPTER THIRTY-THREE

For Ahna

IF YOU'RE VERY LUCKY,
when you gaze into someone's eyes
you will see to the ends of the universe.
Actually much further than that.

It doesn't matter if they are blue or green or brown.
Although if they are a blue that matches Heaven
that seems to help.

It is like a window into infinity,
a doorway into the most Sacred.

You look so far and deep that
you seem to come full circle.
And you end up looking at yourself.

This is a love poem,
but I can no longer tell who it's for.

Is it for Ahna?
Is it for me?
Is it for God?

I don't know.

The Zen of Love

The lines have blurred.

There were once two bodies here.
Now there is only Heaven.

Isn't this what love is?

CHAPTER THIRTY-FOUR

Relationships and Love

HOW DOES REAL LOVE make your relationships wonderful and lasting? First you must not cling to the relationship or to your partner. Put your faith in love instead. And put your faith in real love. Real love is present only in this present moment. It is real, so that's all it can be. It cannot be encased in a memory of the past. That's not real love. It cannot be something you hope for in the future. That is also only a dream. Real love can only exist right now in the present moment. That's where real love is. Anything that is true can only be true now. It cannot be true in the past or future, which actually do not exist.

Real love does not change. It does not grow or fade. Only our awareness of it can grow or fade. You cannot lose it. How much larger than infinite would you want it to be? How much longer than eternity should it be? True love is already complete. It has nothing to gain and nothing to lose. It cannot change, no matter what happens around you. Because true love never changes, you can always put your faith in it. This is something you can put your whole life into and you will never be disappointed. In the dream, everything changes and nothing is reliable.

I know it may be painful to hear this, and you may resist it or even put the book down or fling it across the room. But true love means I must speak truth to you no matter what the consequences. I must say what is true and only what is true. And true love is true. That's why I call it true love to separate it out from the false, limited love of the dream world.

But I have a wonderful secret for you. Even the false and limited love of the dream world has a spark of true love in it. And that makes it a wonderful bridge and guide to awakening. Not only that, true love and learning about true love, as you will in this book, teaches you how to improve your relationships dramatically. You must put true love above all other things. You must put true love above your relationship, and even your partner, and even your own limited idea of a self-concept. Only when you can do this will your relationships be guaranteed to be happy. Your relationships will be happy because you will be happy. You will always have love in your heart, so there is no reason to worry if your relationship will last or not. If your relationship ends, if your partner leaves you or dies, you will still have the greatest gift the world can ever give: and that is True Love. You will be in relationship without fear as so many are. You will be in relationship without neediness. You will be in relationship complete and fulfilled no matter what happens.

You will be a rare person who walks this earth because you will be in the dream and at the same time not in the dream. You will appear to be in the same dream as everyone else, but you will be free. You will be a free person depending on nothing and nobody. You will be complete unto yourself. You will be love. Because you are love you'll attract more partners and friends than you can imagine. Every beautiful woman will want to be your lover. Every handsome man will want to be with you. You will become irresistible. Other awakened people will recognize you instantly. They'll feel your energy and instantly know you.

You'll walk this earth as a true king or queen. You will have a wonderful nobility, but also an even more wonderful humbleness. No longer will you feel the need to feel better than anyone or anything because no longer will you feel separate from anyone or anything. You will be One with the universe. You will be one with God. As God is love, this should not be surprising. All this time you may have thought that God was something different, some superhuman-type figure up in the clouds who judged humans and sent them to heaven or hell, who punished the wicked and rewarded the good. And this is a nice children's fairy tale. But it is a tale meant for children. As an adult, you no longer need to believe this. God is love. That is what God is. And love is everything. And so God is also everything. God and love are not separate. So you see, love is really much more than you might have thought.

Healings happen in the dream world, solely based on love. Miracles of all types really happen in the dream world, all based on but love alone. Only love is real. And the closer you come to this truth, the healthier in all ways you and everyone around you will be.

You might also ask about individuality. Who am I as a person? Does it really matter? You are love. Love has no individuality. And yet it can express itself in an infinite number of different ways. And it does. Your expression of love can be highly individual. In fact, it cannot help but be highly individual. It is your unique expression. But love itself remains the same, unchanging, infinite and eternal. Your expression can vary greatly depending on the need. But love doesn't change. And who you truly are doesn't change even if your expression of love does. So, my Dearest One, you are love. And love is all there is, as I said at the beginning. And if you see this, if you feel this, you will step out of a dream that is no more than a very temporary nightmare, a dream that you are alone in a vast universe, a dream that you are separate from God and this great love that you are. You will step out of this nightmare, what awakened people call hell, and you will step into Paradise, Heaven, the world of True Love.

CHAPTER THIRTY-FIVE

The World of True Love

COME WITH ME and step into the world of True Love. Come with me and be free of all suffering, of all illusions of pain and sorrow. You don't need them any longer. They were a way for you to grow, a way for you to learn what illusion is. And the only reason for doing this was to return Home to the love that you are. That is why these guideposts were given to you. This book is one of them. You have had many others: *A Course in Miracles*, the Bible, the Buddhist Sutras, the *Bhagavad Gita*, and so many teachers and books and teachings, all to help you awaken from this dream.

This dream is very convincing while you are in it. And most of human consciousness is very much in it and believes in it completely. This makes it quite hard to step outside of it. And this is why, for so long, only a few people ever did step out of the dream; only a very few people ever really awakened. We called them the enlightened ones. And they tried to help us wake up too. But very few of us did, even with their very clear help and guidance. In this book I will show you that one of your most common experiences in the dream is the primary way for you to transcend the dream.

You mistake love in the dream for something given to you by another. And this other is someone separate from you. They have a different body and you still believe in bodies. My body is here and my Beloved's body is over there. So you feel separate.

But as your love grows, doesn't this feeling of separation also fade? When you are in the throes of sexual passion, do you not feel sometimes as if the two bodies have merged together into one single body? And this is the beauty of making love. It is a symbol for Oneness, for Truth, for True Love. If you see it as just sex, you will miss what it is really pointing to. It is not just a biological expression of the physical body. It is a spiritual symbol of ultimate oneness. So in this way the sexual act becomes sacred. It becomes holy.

And this is the true meaning of Tantra. We use the everyday things of the dream to move beyond the dream to Truth. In Tantric practice we use the very things that invoke separation in the dream as a way to invoke union with God. All acts, not only sex, can become Tantric: eating, walking, working, singing, everything. But the sexual act can be an extremely powerful doorway. And in this way sex can lead directly to real love and that means directly to God. Who would have thought of this in the dream? And yet for thousands of years, Tantric teachers have taught this very path. It is one of many. But though it is a path to awakening, it can also distract from true love and from God when we place too much emphasis on the tool of awakening: in this case two bodies and the sexual act itself.

This is also true of all spiritual practices. If we become attached to rituals, practices, statues, icons, books, even meditation, we miss that these things are only tools for something far greater. They are tools in the dream that lead out of the dream. And what they lead to is True Love. What they lead to is God.

So True Love in my experience is the best path and practice. It is also the fulfillment of the practice. I don't think you can say that about a single other spiritual practice I know of. Is meditation the fulfillment of the practice? Is chanting mantra the fulfillment to the practice? If so, it is not much of an attainment. If the purpose of meditation is only to be a good meditator, then that's not really much of an attainment. And this is also true of Tantra. If the purpose of Tantric sex is to be good at Tantric sex than this is a pretty limited goal. The purpose of all these things is only for one thing: the Oneness with God – which is True Love.

Oh My Dear One, please come with me to this awakened state. Join me in Paradise. Join me in Heaven on Earth. This is where I live. And you can too. You already do. You just don't know it yet. So come with me and live this way.

Everything is love. That is all there is. And this is the way to live a happy, fulfilled life. I am holy because I am One with God. And this makes that very clear. I am awake because I live in True Love and as True Love. I live in complete connection to God. The dream has faded. It is unimportant. I can see it and act with people in it, but to me I don't believe it. I believe something that cannot be seen with human eyes. I believe in True Love. By True Love I don't mean the true love of the *Princess Bride*, although I love that movie. That is still the love of the dream, but even here there are aspects and glimmers of True Love.

Do not mistake the limited form of love in the dream for what love really is. That is only a dream version of love. And so it must be limited. It must be changeable. It must grow and fade and eventually be lost. You may be married for sixty years, but no matter how good it is, eventually one of you will die. True love cannot ever fade.

I see people all the time who come to me who have beautiful open hearts. They were in an amazing relationship, and then for one reason or another it ended, as sooner or later, everything in the dream must. That's what happens in the dream. And they have become so addicted to the partner who left that they immediately go from great bliss into the most severe depression. What I do is get them to realize that the great love that made them so happy has never really left. It was there before they met their great love. It was there during their wonderful relationship. And it is still here now after he or she has left. In fact it is always here. It is eternal. And usually I can bring them back to this realization. And it is such a relief. It brings so much joy. But soon after they leave me, their mind comes in and creates the same sad story of separation and never finding another love like this again. These are dream stories, and fortunately none of them are true. And yet when we believe them, they create so much misery and suffering in our lives. People have even committed murder or suicide over these false beliefs.

So when we believe the dream, we inevitably encounter great suffering. This may sound strange, but I am also a fan of suffering. Even suffering helps us see through the dream into something much greater. When suffering is intense enough, it can bring us to question the dream itself. If the suffering is intense enough we have no choice. It's either question the dream or descend into the semi-deaths of drug, alcohol or sex addiction, a life of the walking dead. You are technically alive but really just walking dead. If you wonder why zombie movies have become so popular today, it's because the walking dead are a sad reflection of our society. We have become so numb to real life, so disconnected from the truth of life, that we are more dead than alive. And if drugs or alcohol won't do it, there is always the more direct route of suicide.

Zombies may be a popular subject for today's movies, but, please don't become one yourself. There are already far too many walking around, disguised as human beings. Yet inside all of them there is still the spark of life, the spark of real love. It is a tragedy that they have become so numb they can no longer feel it.

But you, My Love, will not be like this. You would not have picked up this book if you were. You've probably seen the people I'm talking about. You may even know some of them. Perhaps they could not take the pain of disillusion we so often face before we wake up. Our entire life and world are radically altered. You no longer see the dream the same way. You're aware other people still live in it, but you no longer do. You are free.

Discover Your Own Awakened Heart

This is who we are. We are pure joy, pure love and pure peace. We are pure freedom. We knew this better when we were children, didn't we? We could roll down a hill all day long and laugh ourselves silly when we were too dizzy to stand up. As children we knew something that adults have forgotten. As adults we forgot who we are. And we became something we manufactured, something we created through our thoughts and beliefs. For the most part these are really other people's thoughts, beliefs, opinions and judgments about us. Parents, friends, teachers, employers, lovers, everyone we have known has judged us in some way, whether good or bad. And all those judgments have gone into a little storage place in our brain, which we now call me. This is who I am. None if it is real. These are nothing but thoughts. It would be one thing if we made the whole thing up ourselves. It's possible that at least some of us would make a happier version of me. But we don't. We are subject to the world of other people's opinions.

The egoic mind creates, protects and defends who we think we are. Because of the very strange way the egoic mind works, we hear, absorb and retain negative comments more than positive ones. Negative comments stick to us like Velcro and we often even filter out the positive comments. This doesn't give us a very good self-image. There is an underlying fear that we're not good enough. Somehow we don't quite measure up to whatever we are measuring. And this is quite sad. So given who we think we are, which is this very limited and not altogether positive creature, why should we believe that we are pure joy, pure peace and pure love? It is obvious that we wouldn't. This is our ego self, unhappy and limited, which actually prefers suffering to happiness.

Happiness is too much like what we really are. So the ego clings to and pays attention to what is the opposite of what we really are. It prefers suffering to happiness. It prefers sickness to health. It may not seem like it to you now, grasped so tightly in the ego's talons, convinced you are this limited self who needs so much protection and defense. But this is true. The ego prefers suffering because suffering reinforces the ego. Suffering reinforces this illusory belief in limitation, smallness, weakness and vulnerability. Happiness, strength, power and love reinforce our belief in who we truly are, which is unlimited, total and unconditional pure love. The ego really doesn't want you to feel these things.

A spiritual teacher was once asked by a student, "I have been listening to you talk for almost four hours and I haven't heard you say one nice thing about the ego. I want to hear you say something good about the ego." The teacher turned to him and said simply, "The ego wants you dead."

And this is really true. The ego wants you dead. The ego doesn't want you to know who you are. The ego doesn't want you happy, at peace, or feeling unconditional love. It doesn't want you free. If you experience these things you move closer and closer to who you truly are. Since you are not the ego and the ego is a very poor substitute for who you really are, once you realize who you are or even get a tiny glimmer of it you will choose the your true self over the ego every time. Who wouldn't?

So let me help you make this choice now. You are unlimited love. That is what and who you are. You are not the limited, vulnerable little self the ego wants you to think you are. Don't believe the ego when it tells you that sometime in the future you can find out who you are and the ego will help you. It will never happen. The ego is totally against you ever discovering who you are. And it is totally against you ever being happy except for moments of pseudo-happiness, the kind of limited and changeable fake happiness that substitutes for real happiness. Fake happiness changes. That's how you know it is fake. You're happy one day, and sad or blah the next. That is fake happiness. True happiness doesn't change. It doesn't vary. It's not here one day and gone the next. Like True Love, it is unchanging, infinite and eternal. Don't put your hope in fake happiness, fake peace or fake love. All these things change. They are nothing but the ego's dream. You don't need them. Real happiness, real peace and real love do not change. They remain just as they always are.

I am Peace. I am Love. I am Happy. And so are you.

CHAPTER THIRTY-SIX

You Are Already Happy. You Were Just Too Busy Arguing to Notice.

IF YOU THINK ABOUT the relationship you are in now, or past relationships, there appear to be some problems, don't they? He doesn't give me enough attention. She does all the talking and never listens. He never expresses his feelings. Not enough sex. Too much sex. She squeezes the toothpaste from the top not the bottom. He always leaves the toilet seat up. Her mother hates me. He's got mommy issues. She's got daddy issues. You probably have your own list of grievances, things you wish were done more or better or not at all.

It's the nature of most relationships to have at least some problems. If you need help, there is an entire industry devoted to helping you with these problems: couples therapy, marriage counseling, books, workshops, couples retreats.

And yet in spite of all these apparent problems and the myriad solutions for them, there is really only one problem. There is one single cause for every one of these and all the other problems couples face in their relationships. This one single problem is the cause of all divorces, all marital discord, and all the unhappiness you have ever experienced in every relationship you have ever been in. And until this one problem is solved, all the books, workshops, retreats and couple's therapy in the world cannot help you.

That one problem is your own ego, your own sense of being a unique, separate person. And here's how it works. Because you feel separate from the world, you feel incomplete. There is always the sense that something is missing. You never feel whole. So you search in the world for things you hope might make you feel more complete. Because you feel lonely in your incompleteness, you search for a partner to make you feel less alone.

People sometimes call this their other half or better half as if without them they are only half a person. And since the ego does feel incomplete, this makes perfect sense to the ego. The problem is that it does not and cannot work. In this case, two halves do not make a whole. Because the ego halves are both illusions, they can only create the illusion of a whole. No person or anything else you find in the outside world will ever make you feel complete. As long as the ego is experienced and believed in, the sense of incompleteness remains. The very nature of the ego is this sense of separation and incompleteness.

In the beginning of the relationship, we experience a feeling of more completeness, happiness and love. This is the falling-in-love phase. It appears to be the other person who is creating this feeling of completeness and happiness. But really it is simply the slipping away of the illusion of the ego and the first small glimpse of the True Self, which is always by nature one hundred percent complete. And even this tiny glimpse is felt as love and happiness, for the True Self is not separate from the loved one or anything else. Love, peace and happiness are the natural experiences of the True Self.

Notice that in the falling-in-love phase, there don't seem to be any problems. It is with the return of the imaginary ego and the felt sense of separation and incompleteness that problems begin. Because the ego feels separate and incomplete, it is always searching for ways to make itself feel more connected and complete. At best, these can only be temporary solutions.

And connection and completeness, along with happiness, peace and love, can only be experienced to the degree that the ego is not experienced. And there's the rub. The ego identifies with one body, one mind, one personality, one past to the exclusion of and separation from everything else. The ego is the sense of separation and incompleteness itself. So any solution in the outside world, including a loving partner, can only be temporary at best. And that temporary solution can only come because the ego has temporarily retreated, and the True Self is allowed to be experienced again.

The Ego and Relationships

Since the ego always feels incomplete, it is always searching for completeness. Since this completeness can never be satisfied as long as the ego is experienced, it is always frustrated. The ego projects this frustration out onto others and the world. To recognize where the frustration and all problems really come from would reveal the ego as it really is, and that would be the beginning of its end. So it must project the frustration out into the world where it is not. When this frustration is projected onto a partner, the relationship appears to have problems. And to the ego, those problems are always and only caused by the partner, who from the ego's point of view is always separate. The partner is not giving or doing enough. Or the partner is doing too much. Or the partner is doing too much of the wrong things, and not enough of the right things. No matter how seemingly insignificant, the ego will project some imagined fault and magnify it.

In truth, nothing is really happening in the relationship. There are no problems. Life is simply being life. Everything is always one hundred percent complete, because who we really are is always one hundred percent complete. Realizing this, even in the most basic and preliminary way, is love. It doesn't mean changes can't be made, but they are made effortlessly in love, peace and happiness instead of conflict. And this is how the True Self engages with life, not as something separate, but in the bliss of Oneness.

The ego is never satisfied because it never feels complete. If one projected problem is solved (he puts down the toilet seat; she listens), a new one will quickly take its place. As long as the ego is still in place, there will always be problems. The very nature of the ego is suffering and the projection of this suffering out onto the world. The ego sees the world as full of problems. The True Self sees the world as perfect and complete just as it is.

One Solution to All Relationship Problems

Since the ego is the cause of all relationship problems, the solution is always to reduce the ego. Our natural state of being is complete. It is happy and complete whether it is in a relationship or not. It does not experience neediness, because it is already complete. Small things do not upset our True Self, nor do big things. It is not separate from all of life, so the comings and goings of life do not disturb it. Where the ego sees many things that need fixing in a relationship, our True Self simply experiences love and the effortless, perfect flow of life.

This does not mean that your only hope is to become completely Enlightened and ego free – although that would be nice. Any reduction of the ego helps. When you first fell in love, your ego was not as strong. This connection with your Beloved helped reduce your attachment to it. You were not completely ego free, yet you experienced the love and happiness that always accompanies the reduction of the ego. You also experienced far fewer (if any) problems in your relationship. Things that later, when your ego re-emerged, drove you absolutely crazy, you barely even noticed then.

It is the ego alone that is creating all the problems you see in your relationship. It is the ego alone that is creating all the problems you see in the world. It is projecting itself, its incompleteness, its frustrations and its suffering onto your partner, your relationship and the world. It doesn't want you to be aware of this. Right now, as you read this, it doesn't want you to see it. It is already resisting. But something else in you sees this and everything else very clearly. Perhaps you should pay attention to that deep inner guidance that speaks from your heart, that sense that everything is okay, everything is complete, everything is already perfect.

The ego has many arguments of why this cannot be. Have you noticed how the ego would rather be right than happy? You only know Truth through the experience of love and happiness, so the ego is never actually right. The ego is only an illusion, a mistaken belief in separation and incompleteness. It is never right because it itself is not true. The next time you feel yourself wanting to win an argument, ask yourself if you would rather be right or happy? If you want to be happy, you will simply stop arguing and be happy. Winning an argument, any argument, can never make you happy. You are already happy. You were just too busy arguing to notice.

CHAPTER THIRTY-SEVEN

Love Is the Only Real Medicine

THE BEST WAY TO DEAL with any illness (physical, emotional or psychological) is to love it. Loving it means you are totally accepting of it and totally present with it. It is being the most accepting and most present you can be with it.

Whatever you love that is not true will dissolve beneath the powerful light of love. But you can't have that as the goal. You must love it exactly as it is, exactly as you experience it in the moment. Then notice how it changes. For instance, "My head hurts." Love that feeling of pain in the head. If it is here, why not love it? Is resistance to it helping you? Is resistance making it feel better? Or is resistance just making it feel worse and more real? That is what resistance does. It always makes things worse. So, instead, love it.

It may be causing terrible pain. Love the pain completely. You can love anything. Love is not only for things you prefer. It is a choice. And when you love it, you also prefer it. It does not matter what it is. You can love sadness. You can love hate. You can love depression. You can love feeling frustrated. You can love the feeling that you cannot love. Make that choice to love whatever is happening, and notice how things change. Love everything in this moment simply because it is in this moment. Love your memories of the past that are occurring in this moment. It doesn't really matter what these memories are: good, bad, horrible, frightening, depressing, intolerable.

Love is the only choice you need to make. You will either love what is or you will resist what is. Loving what is changes everything, unless you are already loving what is.

It is not a question of How you love what is. There is no How. You simply love what is. It is a simple choice. You have been choosing to resist, repress or ignore what is. Occasionally, if something wonderful happens, you love what is for a little while, like maybe seeing a beautiful sunset. This is also a choice, just not a conscious one. So I am saying consciously choose to love what is, all the time. Simply make that choice. Start with the things you usually resist – depression, illness, sadness, anger, fear. This is wonderful. Then the more neutral things will be much easier. Just make this choice. Focus on one thing at a time until you love it completely. Soon it will be easy to simply love all of it completely, everything. This is also what it feels like to be awake. Make this simple choice. It will not only cure your illness, but it will lead you to your natural state of being. That's just another word for being awake.

Smile

To help with loving everything, just smile. You don't need a reason to smile. Just smile. Love and joy actually have no reasons. They are simply here all the time as our basic nature. We imagine they need reasons, but this is just another of our illusions, a way of choosing to cover up what we are. Stop covering up your never-ending unconditional joy and love. Purposely choose to let it free again.

At first this will seem to take effort to make this choice. This is because you have such a long habit of making the opposite choice – resistance. This is the most common in our conditioned culture. But it doesn't make it real or sane. It simply makes it "normal" for an insane culture. Choosing love and joy is really the only sane way you can live. It is simply being your natural self. It doesn't matter that 99.9% of humans do not do this, at least here in the western world. That's not your business. Allow them to suffer until they have had enough suffering and decide to wake up. Then you can help them. You will know when that time is. And your own endless, unconditional love and joy is already helping them. So just claim this now. Make this simple choice. The effort you will make in the beginning is only an effort to stop doing what you have been doing. Stop resisting. You do this by consciously doing the opposite. Resisting resistance will not help. You do this by consciously loving. Consciously loving everything. Consciously love resistance.

You do this by consciously smiling to reflect the inner joy that is always here. It will take a little practice to stop doing what you have been habitually doing for so long, choosing to resist what is. So now consciously choose to love what is. Eventually you will no longer have to choose, as you will naturally return to your natural state – which is love and joy. And you will realize that all these things you are resisting have never been separate from you. If they are illusions they will naturally dissolve, and you will realize they are illusions you created, never separate from you in any way. Even the illusion that they are separate and something you actually could resist is an illusion you created. Love is the way through all of this. So just make that choice. And, as I'm sure you can now imagine, you will start feeling pretty damn good. Our only real suffering comes entirely from not knowing who we really are, and believing there is actually any separation anywhere. That's what suffering is. We give it a thousand names: headache, depression, anxiety, grief, anger, disease. But there has always been only one cause. And each of these appearances (names) of suffering can lead us back to that single cause, if we are willing to look at it. Looking means embracing, not resisting. Looking means loving.

I have a friend who was a very successful and popular doctor, working in the ER of a major Boston hospital. One night, as a complete surprise to him since he was only forty-two years old, he suffered a severe heart attack and was rushed to the same hospital and ER where he worked. He had worked with many heart-attack patients, but this time he himself was the patient. This time it was his pain. He was frightened and felt very alone. The staff was especially attentive to him, as they are whenever a doctor is admitted to the hospital, and one young nurse asked if there was anything she could do for him. The only thing he could think of was to ask her to hold his hand while they waited for an operating room to open up. This simple act of human kindness is not usually available in today's busy ERs. But my friend was a doctor, and well liked at the hospital.

What he needed more than anything in that moment was human connection. In this high-tech, state-of-the-art hospital, what he needed more than anything was love. The operation was successful. But my friend said that he would not have survived without that simple expression of love, which is so rarely offered in today's modern hospitals. That one experience changed forever the way he dealt with his patients. More than anything else, my friend credits this one act of caring, given by this one young nurse, for saving his life. Anyway you look at it, it always comes back to love. If you have read this far, this should no longer come as a surprise.

CHAPTER THIRTY-EIGHT

The Song Of Love

THE HEART MUST BE SINGING in order for you to hear its song. Listen. Listen to its song. And maybe your heart will respond and sing back. I promise I will hear it. But you don't have to speak or write. Your heart will simply vibrate with the resonance of the song my heart is singing right now. That is all.

That is how your heart will sing in harmony with mine. So simply allow your heart to respond to these words, and to the energy flowing along with them. Simply allow your heart to respond, to resonate, to vibrate with this frequency of love that is carried in these words – this love that is also all around you and within you.

So please listen to my Heart Song, My Song of Love. And I will hear your response. I will hear the sweet harmony we make together just as you will. Can you feel it even now? Can you feel the vibration of your heart? I want this for you. This Heart Song is how we awaken from this dream of death and sadness and illusion. These vibrating heartstrings are how we wake up. And you, My Love, are already awake. You, My Love, have felt this same tremor of the Heart before. Oh yes, you have felt the Heart vibrate like this so many times, and in so many ways. It has been with you all your life. Sometimes you are not aware and you imagine your heart is sleeping. But your heart never sleeps, not even when your body is sound asleep. Your heart is still vibrating, still trembling, with its sweet, infinite and eternal song. It has never slept.

Dear One, please believe me that my heart is filled with love for you. And that my heartstrings are vibrating with every word of love I speak to you. And this love you cannot help but vibrate with. Everywhere people are feeling this calling, this vibration of the heart. And isn't this what Krishna's flute is really about? Isn't it this same vibration of the Heart? The internal longing so deep that we often no longer even feel it. So deep and powerful that we can no longer bear to be aware of it. That is how strong this calling is. That is how strong the pull of the Heart is. It says always, "Wake up. Wake up, My Dearest One. It is time. Wake up." Even in the midst of the dream it never stops calling you. It is you who have stopped listening to its call.

Your mind has mistakenly believed that this one call can never be answered. Your mind has convinced you that this one call, your very deepest desire and longing, can never be answered. It can never be fulfilled. And so you have stopped listening. You stopped hearing its call because you felt it would never happen, not such a deep eternal and infinite love. So you stopped listening and you settled for a pale imitation. You settled for the dream of fame, wealth, success, material accumulation, sex or romance. You settled for a tiny, limited version of this great and glorious love that you, My Beloved Child, are. You settled for gray when all the colors of the rainbow surround you. So in this black-and-white world, this world of muted grays, you struggled and lived and died. You did this, lifetime after lifetime. But now the real world has come to you again. The Calling has begun again. And it is right here in this book. Not only in this book – it is everywhere you look.

It is in the sound of crickets and tree frogs on a summer night, the song of the first birds in the morning, the contagious laugh of a child. Can you hear it calling you once again? It has truly never stopped calling your name, My Love. Just as I am calling you right now, your heart has never stopped calling. And all around you in every moment of your life we are calling you home. You, the True Self of you, is calling you Home to this one, single, greatest-of-all Truths. You are what you have been longing for. You are this great, infinite and eternal love that you have sought for so long. This is truly what you are. And you have never really ever been anything different, no matter what you had thought. And more than this, everything in your dream has actually been pointing you back to this one single thing. You just didn't know it. So distracted by the dream were you that you just didn't realize it.

Your life, just like mine, is a river of love endlessly flowing. It has flowed for lifetime after lifetime. And yet you mistook it for something else. The whole dream world mistook it for something else. And this dream world was built of opposites: of love and hate, of war and peace, of good and bad, of hatred and kindness, of beauty and ugliness. It is a world of seeming opposites. It is a world of competition, of haves and have-nots, of great wealth and debilitating poverty. And all of these seeming opposites were so convincing because you had forgotten who you are, and so you believed it. You believed what you were seeing. You believed the dream.

But it has never been like this, My Child. It has never been like this. And so you suffered. And so you tried and failed. And so you succeeded, then found that what you attained was as empty as the dream itself because it was never anything but a dream. And this is how your life went, lifetime after lifetime.

Buddha called this the wheel of Samsara. You are born again and again, until you finally wake up and see that it was all a dream. It doesn't mean you leave the physical world. It simply means you leave the dream. Buddha didn't leave the physical world to awaken. Jesus didn't leave the physical world. And neither shall you. You will awaken from the dream, right here where you are.

CHAPTER THIRTY-NINE

A Special Gift

MY DEAR ONE, I have a special gift for you today. Right now as you are reading this, I am going to bring the Light of God into the room you are sitting in. I am going to fill your room with the Light and Love of God. I am going to fill the room and you, so that every cell in your body is activated and pulsing with the glorious Light of God. This Light is so powerful that it will instantly wash clean any thoughts or remnants of illness, sadness, despair, hopelessness, or doubt.

Yes, this is so. I have always done this before in person, but now today I am doing it through only the written word, and the energy of Truth and Love it carries with it.

You may be thinking, how is this possible? Or who does he think he is? And this is because you do not see who I am. You do not see me. You think I am simply Peter, a person, one who struggles with life just as you do. And in our common dream of separation (mass hypnosis), this is so. But I am not talking from this dream now. I cannot help you in this dream. I cannot offer you the Light of God in this dream, for the Light of God does not exist here in our imaginations. It is much more real and present than that.

And yet still, right this very moment, the Light of God is filling your room, filling every single particle of your being. You may not understand it, but somehow you can feel it. There is an aliveness in your very cells, an energy in your body you cannot explain. Do not fight it. Do not try to understand it. Simply allow it. It only means the ultimate in care and love. You can also think of this Light as Pure Love, and you would not be wrong. There is nothing I have ever experienced that heals the way this does. So allow it to find what needs healing on its own. There is no reason to direct Infinite Intelligence. You cannot know what It Knows.

And yet something inside you does Know. Your mind cannot understand This. But Something Else does Know. And It has always Known. And this is why I can say I know that this is happening right now, right as you read this. Because I am there too. I am right there with you. Or should I say here because there is only really Here. And I can say I know this because there is only really One.

And this Light, this Pure Infinite Unconditional Love, that right now is flowing freely through every cell in your body, is You. It has always been Here. Your body could not be alive for a single instant if this were not so. So I am not really bringing anything. You are doing it. The True You. You are doing all of it. And You are always Here. This Healing Light of Truth and this Unfathomable Infinite Love is not only filling your room and your body and mind and heart, it is everywhere. And it always has been. It is the Light of God. It is the Love of God. It is God. It is with you right Now. And it has never been separate from you. You are One with It.

My gift is only to remind you of this. My gift today is only to remind you of something that Deep Inside you already Know and have always Known. As a Healer, that is all I have ever done.

You may experience some resistance to this. That is fine. That is what the mind does. It is quite natural for the mind to resist something of this magnitude, of a Truth that is so far beyond the dream it cannot be imagined. But there is also an Inner Knowing, a Deep Feeling that Knows on a very visceral level that this is all True. The one that wins is the one you feed.

Discover Your Own Awakened Heart

So for just a moment, right now, allow this healing to happen. Somehow I know you will. You have no idea just how blessed and loved you are. But you may be starting to feel just a little of it right now.

CHAPTER FORTY

Love and Fear

THERE IS ONLY ONE THING keeping you from experiencing this great love that is in you and all around you. And that is fear. Love means letting go of your boundaries, your borders, your hard edges. It means letting go of everything that separates you from me and the rest of the world. And fear is the opposite of that. Fear is protecting these imagined boundaries and borders, and those hard edges that you believe is who you are. And this is also the cause of all your suffering.

For just a moment, let go. For just a moment, let those boundaries, borders and hard edges dissolve. You can always bring them back again whenever you want. But for now, try something a little different.

Dissolve.

Dissolve this sense of being a separate person with a certain identity. For just a moment, let go and experience what happens. You may be afraid to do this, but for just a moment try anyway. Simply let go. Let go of your fear. Let go of that nervousness. Let go of your thoughts. Let go of you, the you that you believe you are. For just a moment let go of all of it. See what it's like to simply be. Not to be this or that. But to simply be.

Notice how relaxed your body feels. Notice how, where there might have previously been tensions in the body, they no longer seem to be here. Isn't that nice? And notice something else. Notice how good you feel. I mean really, really good. With all the effort you had been putting into being a this or a that, all that effort trying to protect and maintain this identity, you have forgotten what it feels like to feel really, really good. To feel really good for no reason at all, just simply being. And now, perhaps for the very first time in your life, you are beginning to understand what happiness is. You are beginning to experience real peace. You are beginning to feel what love really feels like.

And it is so easy. It is so effortless. You don't have to earn or deserve any of it. It is simply what you are when you are not trying to be something else. Being a person takes a great deal of effort. Being who you really are takes no effort at all. And yet, here is everything you have every really wanted, everything you have searched for. Here is everything you thought you could earn, deserve or attain as a person. Peace, love, happiness. It has been right here all along. Relax. Simply be. Enjoy.

CHAPTER FORTY-ONE

A Love Letter

MY DEAREST, DEAREST CHILD, please be with me on this journey. Please see who you are. For you are no other than me. That is why my love for you is so strong and so complete. You fill my heart completely because you are my heart completely, just as I am yours. You may see this book as a love letter to you. And you would not be wrong.

It can bring you to the full awakening, the full enlightenment you have longed for, for many lifetimes. It can bring you to the infinite and eternal love of God you have never been separate from.

It can solve any relationship problems you have ever had or will ever have. On a practical level, it will teach you how to navigate the tricky road of love in the world of the dream. But it can do so much more than that. It can help lead you out of the dream world entirely into a world where love is the only thing that is real and never changes. It can do this for you if you simply read, listen and open your heart to what you will find in these pages.

For you already know all of these things. Deep in your heart you know that everything you will read in this book is true, and true on the very deepest levels that you know. Your heart has always known this. But for so long you have not listened to your heart. You may have been afraid, if you followed your heart's true longing, so deep and intense is it that if you were disappointed, you would surely not be able to live through this dis-

The Zen of Love

appointment. And this is true. Such a disappointment would be impossible to live through. Every molecule of your being longs for this true love. And if you tried to reach it and failed, the disappointment would be so great it would surely kill you.

What you do not know is that you cannot be disappointed. You cannot possibly not reach this goal, because this is a true goal. And as a true goal it has already been fulfilled.

Your dream goals are illusions, and they will always disappoint you, as you are already learning. It doesn't matter if it is career, relationship or success: eventually you will be disappointed because illusions, since they are not real, can never offer lasting happiness. Only what is real can offer lasting happiness. But in your great good fortune, love does turn out to be real. Your own greatest longing is for something that is very real, unchanging, infinite and eternal. And that is true love. Your heart has always known this. Deep in your heart, deep in this greatest longing, you also know even deeper that what you are seeking is what you already are, have always been, and could never, under any circumstances, not be. And that is the great secret and great blessing of life. You are love. And your very deepest longing is already fulfilled. It is already complete. The search is already over before it even began. But you don't know this yet. You are still in the game. You will learn this in your own perfect time and your own perfect way. Picking up this book was also part of the game. It was one of the many breadcrumbs you scattered to help you find your way back Home. You could even say you wrote this book you are reading now to help you find your way back Home. You would not be wrong in this.

Only in the dream do you not yet understand this. But deep in your own heart you do know. So I am only reminding you, Dear One. I am only asking you to wake up and listen to your heart. Your heart has never been silent. But you have not been listening. The world of the dream is filled with distractions. And much of it is so convincing, intriguing, seductive and often

Discover Your Own Awakened Heart

horrifying.

This is not just a path you are on, but also the completion of the path. I am only asking you to awaken to what you already are. And this is so wonderful. This is Heaven Itself. This is God Itself. I am only asking you to wake up to what you already are – to wake up to love.

And if you read this book carefully – not only the words, but the feeling and energy that travel with these words – you will wake up. Already you can feel the pull of your heartstrings.

My Dearest One, my Heart is filled with love. And so I send this love to you so that you too may know what it is like to be fully awake to this beautiful, glorious world, this world of divine true love.

You may have mistaken what real love is. You may have not realized that in each and every experience of love there is a spark of true love, of divine love. And this also means a spark of God. What you take for love in the dream is but a pale imitation of what real love is. You look at your object of affection, and believe that this is the true cause of your love. So if something changes and he or she leaves or dies, you are shattered. You believe that love has left you.

So attached are you to the form, that you miss the true experience of love that you feel swelling in your heart. You do not realize that this feeling of love is always here. It is here before you met your Beloved, during the time you were with your Beloved, even during fights, and after your Beloved has gone. In fact, this true experience of love has never left you, nor could it ever leave you, because it is in fact what you are. It is your True Self. Your True Self is love.

This True Love is always with you. I've helped many people through broken hearts when a loved one leaves them or dies, by helping them experience that the great love they felt for their loved one at the very height of their relationships is still here right now, even years after they have gone. And this is true healing.

CHAPTER FORTY-TWO

Death Does Not End True Love

YES, EVEN DEATH does not end true love. True love is just as present after death as it was before. I am old enough to have experienced many deaths of loved ones: my father, grandfather, my brother, grandmother, my dear friends. And in each and every case, the essence of that person has never left me They are just as alive to me now in Spirit as they were when they were alive in their physical bodies.

So love has taught me the illusion of death. Death cannot exist because these people have all physically died. There is no longer a body. But it is very clear that they have never gone anywhere. And my love for them has never abated or even changed, just as their love for me has never changed. This is the power of true love. It is more powerful than even death. And it shows that the physical death of the dream world does not really exist at all.

While my loved ones were alive in their bodies, I was often under the common illusion that we were separate beings. If they were not with me physically, I felt we were separated. If I had not seen them for some time, I would miss them. I felt we were only together if they were physically in my presence. But with the death of their physical body, this illusion vanished. The illusion of two separate beings disappeared, and I realized deeply that we had never been separate. You might even say that the death of their body made us closer, because it ended the illusion of our separation. And this is why I do not mourn when a loved one passes. I feel their being as my own with no separation at all. In the past I might have only felt connected to them when we were physically together or speaking on the phone. Now I realize I am connected to them always, and always have been. It was only the appearance of a separate body and personality that caused me to think otherwise. No matter where anyone is in the world, they cannot be separate from me.

And this is just as true for you. If you have lost a loved one and are grieving, let me help you. You can call me or email me and I will help you see that they have never really left you. They are still with you now, as much a part of you as what you believe to be you. Love shows us that there can be no separation.

The dream shows us that everything is separate. You are not your beloved, not your parents, not your children. You are not the tree in your backyard or your neighbor or your neighbor's barking dog. You are not any of those things. You are distinctly separate from all of them. But love shows that this is not true. It is only a dream. You are intimately One with all of these things, and everything and everyone else you now perceive as being separate from you. This is the truth of life, and it is how you see life once you awaken from the dream. It is a beautiful world when the dream of separation has been removed from your consciousness. And it is only love that can do this. For love really means when you get right down to it, there is no separation. No separation from anything. No separation from anyone.

Love guides us from within the dream to wake up from the dream. In each and every experience of love there is a taste of true enlightenment. Love is both the path to enlightenment, the bridge to enlightenment and enlightenment itself.

Since we are in a dream, we mistake it for the dream version of love – which is limited, changeable and temporary, just like everything else in the dream. True love is outside the dream and can never change. It is eternal and infinite and the most powerful thing in existence. And yet here in the dream of separation, of suffering and misery and striving, we have these little tastes of Paradise, these little tastes of Heaven. Some of us give up seeking love early because we have had such bad experiences with the limited, changeable dream version of love. But that is not what this book is about, although we do talk about the dream versions of love and help you bridge from those unsatisfactory experiences to the permanent bliss of true love. This book is really about True Love, which is infinite and eternal, and not separate from God.

This book is about that love. And it will guide you step by step to seeing that this love has really always been in your life. Even when you thought your heart was breaking from the dream version of love, true love was still right here. You were so distracted by the dream that you could not see what was really happening. When you awaken, you will see that really the only thing that has actually ever existed is love. It is that pervasive. The dream shows many different things. What it never shows is true love, because true love is the end of the dream. The dream and true love cannot coexist. Once you experience true love, you can no longer believe in the dream.

CHAPTER FORTY-THREE

The Rose And You

A ROSE IS NOT UNLIKE YOU. You are a young bud in your mother's womb. Nine months later you blossom. And this blossom grows and evolves for eighty or ninety years. And then it fades. The petals dry out and fall to the ground. Eventually the entire appearance of the rose is gone. And this is just like the rose, blossoming in springtime and fading or falling in autumn.

Yet even in the midst of winter, when the thin stalks of the rose bush are covered in snow and ice and nowhere is the beautiful red of the rose seen, there is still the essence of the rose. You may not see it with your physical eyes, but if you are aware, you can still sense that it is here. The essence of the rose cannot die. It does not come and go. It does not bloom and fade. And this is just like you.

Your body may form in your mother's womb. Nine months later it may emerge and let out its first cry. It may grow into the strong and vibrant flower of a young man or woman. It may experience many things on its journey through this life. And after eighty or ninety years it will fade. It will fall back to the earth, just as the rose flower does. And isn't this really why we love roses and all flowers so much? We can see that they are us. They blossom and fade just like us, but much quicker – so we can be aware of this beautiful process of life.

Most people only see the rose after it has blossomed. They are captivated by its deep red color and beautiful perfume. They are not so aware of the new bud, and they may even experience a moment of sadness or disappointment when the beautiful red fades and the petals fall to the ground. Fewer people are aware of the essence of the rose that neither blossoms nor fades, but is always here.

And this is just as true of our awareness of ourselves and each other. We may be aware of the bud growing in a mother's womb, or at least the strong potential of this human flower. But we cannot see it. We are not really aware until we do. We are just using our imaginations. Even an ultrasound scan doesn't give us a very accurate picture. The moment of birth nine months later is our blossoming. We can call it that, because this is the first time we are seen by human eyes. And this is the time most humans are aware of us. Most humans do not see beyond the limitations of their physical eyes. And even fewer are aware of our presence when the human body has faded and can no longer be seen. When it is cremated or buried in the earth, our loved ones cry because they do not see the essence. They feel that when the body has died the one they love has also died. But just like the rose, this cannot be. The essence remains. It can neither come nor can it go. Before this essence was a fertilized egg in its mother's womb, it was here. Before the birth of its physical parents, this essence was still here. Before this planet and solar system were more than random space dust, the essence of you and me and the rose was still here. It is here now and it will always be here.

If we have eyes to see, we can see the rose in the middle of winter. Not just in our imaginations, but we can really see it. We can see its essence. If we have eyes to see and a heart that knows, we can see our loved ones long after their bodies are no longer in view. This is not imagination. This is simply awareness. As *A Course in Miracles* says, "Nothing real can be threatened. Nothing unreal exists. Herein lies the peace of God." When we find what is real we will find the essence, the source of all that is. We will find what does not change, what can never

Discover Your Own Awakened Heart

change – and all our problems and suffering will be over.

It may be too challenging for you to see this in a human or in yourself right now. That's fine. Begin with a rose. It is a good place to start. And it is no different than you are. When you can see its essence, you will know this is true – and you will be very happy.

CHAPTER FORTY-FOUR

Exercise - Feeling Love Everywhere

FOR A MOMENT, RELAX. Take a few deep breaths. Focus your attention inside, in the center of your chest. Let all your other thoughts go and just pay attention to what you feel here, in the center of your chest. Can you feel that? Can you feel something stirring? Can you feel some energy moving?

It feels good, doesn't it? Focus on this feeling for a while. Allow it to grow. Don't direct or control, simply allow and observe. Take your time. Let it move at its own pace.

Let this feeling of love expand in your chest, expand in your heart. Feel it filling the entire chest area. Feel it moving down past your chest to your stomach, out to your shoulders, through your arms and fingers. Feel it moving up into your neck and filling your head, your face, your mouth, your jaw, your nose, your eyes, your forehead, your ears, and now your entire skull. And now feel it moving down through your hips and belly and legs and feet. Feel it spill over everywhere.

Feel it in your lungs. Feel yourself breathing love with every single breath. Feel your heart radiating love. Feel your belly filled with love. Feel your hips full of love. Feel your legs, your knees, your calves, your feet and toes. Feel your fingers tingling with the energy of love. Feel that energy permeating every cell of your body. With each in-breath, breathe in love from the universe. With each out-breath, breathe out love to the entire universe.

You are One with everything. You are One. You are love. You are nothing but love. What else could you be? What else could you ever want to be but this enormous love, infinite and eternal? Why would you want to be anything but this? I think now you are getting it. Now you are feeling the love of God, the love of the universe, the love of you. Tell me right now: can you really imagine that there is anything else?

Allow this deep and expanding feeling and awareness of love to continue growing past your body. Let your awareness of love spill out past the imaginary confines of your body to the chair you are sitting on or the floor you are standing on. Allow it to spill out to the walls and everything in the room. Can you feel how really everything in your room is filled and permeated with the power of love? And it is in more than this room. Let your awareness of love grow. Realize that love is not growing. Love never grows. How could it? It is already everywhere. It has no place else to go. It is complete and full and infinite.

Past all space and time there is love. There is always love. It is only your awareness of this that has grown. Allow your awareness to grow so that you become more and more aware of just how infinite love is. Allow your awareness to expand past your room to your entire house, to the street outside your house, to your neighbors' houses, to the town or city you live in. Is there any place in your town or city where love is not present? Can there be any place where love is not present?

Expand your awareness to your entire state. It is an imaginary border. It doesn't really exist. But this is what you now believe, so let your awareness continue throughout all the cities and towns in your state until you are fully aware that love is everywhere present here in this state.

Now realize that it fills this country. It fills this world. Love is in every molecule in every plant. It is in every drop of water in every ocean, pond, lake and river. There is nowhere that love is not. Let your awareness expand, on past the Earth's surface,

Discover Your Own Awakened Heart

into the space that surrounds this beautiful planet we call home.

Notice that love also fills the sun and the other planets that surround us here on Earth. Do you think love could be absent here? No, throughout the entire universe as far as your mind can imagine and far beyond that, throughout the furthest galaxies and furthest star systems, there is love. There is nowhere where love is not.

Now allow your awareness to slowly come back, little by little, back to our universe. Allow your awareness to come back to our solar system, back to our planet, the country, the state, the city, the neighborhood, the house, the room, and finally back to this body that is now aware of just how vast love is.

Now ask yourself, has there ever truly been any single moment in your life when love could ever be absent? Yet you have thought there was. You have believed it completely that there were definitely times when love was quite absent. There have been times when you felt terribly alone and lonely. There may have been times when your best friend or loved one abandoned you, left you or died. You have felt terribly lonely without love. When a loved one died you may have felt as if love had left you too. But I ask you now, as your awareness of love has grown past what you had believed before, if this could really be true? Could this really be true? Could you really be without love then or at any other time, or could you ever be without love in the future?

If you now realize, as I do, that this is impossible, I ask you to feel what you feel right now. Feel the gratitude, the inner happiness that this awareness brings you. You can never be alone. You can never be without love.

So I ask you to be aware of love, and where it is and what it is. I ask you to let your awareness grow beyond the limited dream version of love that you may have thought was love. I ask you for just a moment to let go of this dream of love you learned from television commercials, movies, books, parents and religious teaching. Love is really much more than what can be contained in any teaching, even mine. The true teaching of love can only come from your own heart. So please listen to your own heart. Feel deeply into your own heart and ask a few questions. Can love ever be absent from me? Can love ever not be in my heart? Can my heart ever feel pain? Can love ever lead to pain or suffering or what we had previously called heartbreak?

I think you will get the answer that it cannot. Heartbreak is only caused by a misunderstanding of love. In the dream world, love can hurt. In the world of illusion our hearts can be broken, or feel broken. But that pain is really only the illusion itself. It is only the dream that causes pain. In the real world, the awakened world, the world of the Awakened Heart, there is no pain. There is no suffering. There is not even the chance of a broken heart. That can only come from illusion – the belief that you are a limited person – someone who is only a body or a mind and will live for eighty or ninety years and then die. That is the belief of the dream, for you are nothing like this. You do not resemble this in any way at all. You are unlimited. You are eternal. You are infinite. And you are magnificent beyond any words that I or anyone else can write. That is who you truly are. For you are love itself. And there is nothing greater than real love.

CHAPTER FORTY-FIVE

What Is Awakening? What Is Enlightenment?

YOU ARE SPIRIT. You are no longer a body or a mind or a personality. You are no longer someone with a name or a form or feelings or thoughts. You are free. You are no longer in a body; the body is in you as are all things. You have no limitations. You are not large or small. You are not bound by anything. Some people call this state pure awareness or pure consciousness.

Does consciousness or awareness have a form? Does it have a body? Is it large or small? It all depends where the intention and attention is. That is all. Where are you located in space? You are anywhere and everywhere at once. Is it strange that Spirit can be everywhere at the same time? Where you put your attention you are. If you want to place your awareness on the other side of the planet, you do so instantly. And you are there. And at the same time you are here with this body. We call this bilocation. But to be honest, since we are really everywhere all the time, that is not such an accurate word. This is not some cheap parlor trick. This is simply who and what you are.

When they say that God created man in his image, this is what they really mean. God did not create man in the image of man. And God is not created in the image of man as most humans think, an infinitely large, powerful man somewhere in the sky. That is just a children's fairy tale. "God is watching you, you'd better be careful. You'd better be on your best behavior." That is not God. God doesn't watch you. God is you. God is the real you. Since you are made in the image of God, you too are everywhere. You are omnipresent. You are omnipotent, all powerful. You create entire universes with your thoughts alone. And you are pure spirit. You cannot be bound or defined.

When Socrates said to know yourself, this is what you know. It cannot be defined or described, even by you to yourself. It is too vast for that. It is far too unlimited. If you say one thing, the opposite may be just as true. So you simply say nothing, not even to yourself. And yet there is this great freedom. No longer identified with the body, you are aware of it. You can take care of it. It is a beautiful vehicle for expressing this pure Spirit, the Heart of God, the Voice of God. You have no agenda of your own. You only have God's agenda, for you are not other than God. Nothing is other than God. All the people you see are also like that. You know they see themselves as people, as limited body/minds with stories and histories based on being a physical body, personality and mind. You are totally aware of this. And you know that you once felt this way too. But now you no longer do. You are free. You are awake. And you also know that you are no different from these Spirits that still think they are humans and limited to this human form. So this body that people call you, and give it a name, this body is a wonderful vehicle for communicating. And even this body somehow seems different from other bodies. It has taken on this pure freedom, this complete relaxation and confidence. Since it no longer has anything to prove, it can simply be its natural self. And it can be naturally healthy. Without previous worries and stress, it is free to be healthy as it naturally is. It takes care of itself. But your energy, the energy of pure Spirit that animates all bodies, is now free to express itself in this body.

No body could live a single instant without being animated

by Spirit. It is more important to a body than air, blood, food or water. No body could exist for a single instant without Spirit animating it. When you are identified now as this pure, unbounded Spirit, the body does not resist or have stress or tension. So Spirit now flows freely through it, as it does in a very young child before body identity begins. And this creates abundant natural health. It is the way all bodies are meant to be. But after a time, our thoughts and identifications, our feelings of being limited to a body, take over and our body becomes tense and afraid. We develop fear and stress. And these block the natural flow of Spirit through the body. And after some time of this, illness begins to develop in the body. When you identify as Spirit, this illness goes away. The body is no longer important except as a communications vehicle, which it is perfect for, so you take care of it. But you no longer identify with it since you now identify with something much greater and freer. When the body dies, you remain just as you are, pure freedom, pure Spirit. Nothing really changes at all. And this is so beautiful and wonderful. This is what it means to be outside the dream.

And what does this have to do with love? Love is that feeling of freedom, expansion, being without boundaries, Oneness. Can you put love in a box? Can you describe the boundaries of love? Is love limited to your loved one or your body? It is everywhere, just as you are. Love is not limited, just as Spirit is not limited, just as God is not limited. So love, God and you are all the same. This realization, not as a thought but as a direct experience, is what awakening is all about. You are completely free. You are as God created you. You have always been this, but for a time you simply forgot. The whole human world forgot, and, in their forgetting, became very confused.

So suffering emerged as it had to. Pain and pleasure emerged. Limitations emerged. All of this came about simply because humans forgot who they are. It is not a big thing, and yet it is a very big thing. The whole of human culture is based on nothing but this forgetting. And love is what can bring us back to who we are. In this human dream world, this world of forgetting, there is love. We experience love. And because we experience love, we experience God, we experience Spirit, and we experience our True Self.

This is why I say that love can lead us home. And what does love lead us home to? You could say love itself. You could also call it God. Or you could call it your True Self. All of this would be true, for there is no separation in God. There is no separation in love. There is no separation in you. How does it feel to be awake? It feels free. It feels wonderful. It feels like bliss, peace and love, but on such a deep level that you might not even call it these things any longer. They are the bedrock of your experience. Everything is filtered through this truth. And this truth feels exactly like peace, love and bliss on an incredibly deep level, because this feeling of peace, love and bliss does not change. It is always the same. It is always here. It does not come and go. This is what it means to be awake.

CHAPTER FORTY-SIX

Expand the Circle

JUST OUT OF COLLEGE, I was working at a counseling center for troubled kids. One of the kids came to see me three times a week. He was thirteen. Both parents were alcoholic. His mother had died six months earlier from alcohol poisoning. She basically overdosed on alcohol. He felt totally responsible because his job was to be a parent for his two parents. He had been doing this since he was seven years old. It was a terrible situation. He was living with his father, who was very violent.

There were many similarities to the way I grew up, although not quite as extreme. I connected to this boy very strongly: in the eyes of the therapeutic profession, much too strongly. I loved him. And this created some confusion and conflict because in the eyes of the therapeutic profession this was not supposed to happen. It's called transference. I saw myself in him. This makes it very difficult to do one's job in an impartial and objective way. I cared too much.

I was only in my early twenties, but I already had young children of my own. I was divorced and doing my best to take care of them too. The head of the agency said I had a very serious decision to make about this young boy. I had to recommend removing him from his home and his violent, alcoholic father, and moving him to foster care. I knew that the foster care system in this city was terrible, often not much better than the home he was in now. When I expressed this, the agency head

The Zen of Love

said, "Maybe you should adopt him." I don't think he was serious. He was just trying to help me make a decision to move him to foster care. But I did take it seriously. I was already challenged, taking care of and supporting my own children. But somehow this young boy entered the circle of love too.

I didn't know how I could afford it. I thought it might interfere with my caring for my existing children, and this made me feel guilty. So I didn't do it. It was probably impractical anyway. And even against the ethics of being his counselor/therapist. So I felt confused and disturbed by the situation.

But love itself never feels confused or disturbed. And love is never wrong. Bringing this young boy into the circle of my heart and loving him was not wrong at all. It was entirely natural. It is what love does. In spite of what the therapeutic profession recommends, it should have been done, and should be done, with every client, with every person, with the entire planet. Love should not be reserved for only those who fit into a certain category. You love your beautiful wife or girlfriend, but not the homeless man who is muttering to himself and cursing you. This is the kind of categorization we do in our life. We have an imaginary circle of love. Some are inside the circle, the approved and accepted ones. And others are outside the circle. And society condones this. We have been conditioned to believe that this is normal. And so we suffer. And society suffers. We create circles of suffering.

You may say I love my husband or wife, my children and friends, but those Muslim terrorists or Nazi skinheads or the neighbor who always plays his stereo way too loud and all night long when I'm trying to sleep – there is no way they are coming into my circle of love. And how does that make you feel? How much happiness do you feel by keeping some people out of your circle of love? Not much. Not any. You grumble about them when you think of them. "I can't believe they could do such a thing. What is wrong with them? Why can't they be normal like me?" And you don't feel happy. You don't feel

Discover Your Own Awakened Heart

peace. You don't feel love. This is what it means to keep people outside the circle of your heart, your circle of love.

But it doesn't have to be this way. Just bring one person who is outside your heart into it, and everything changes. Take the noisy neighbor who is keeping you up at night with the loud stereo. It doesn't matter if he turns it down or not, you can still bring him into your circle of love. Just try it and see what happens. Feel what happens. Real love has no expectations. Just love him. Where there was suffering and anger and despair, now there is peace, happiness and love. It is interesting how powerful this simple choice is. But you won't know until you do this. If you are still feeling even a twinge of unhappiness, you have not brought him fully into the circle of your heart yet.

Now that you love your neighbor, go knock on his door and explain the situation. Ask him if he could turn the stereo down or use headphones. You might want to bring him a gift. After all, you do love him now. Very often you will find that the situation changes for everyone's benefit. You may even become close friends with him. If he slams the door in your face, take a deep breath. This is a little more challenging. But love him anyway. And notice how you change. Would you rather feel upset, hurt and angry? Would you rather keep these feelings going by calling your best friend or therapist and complaining? Or would you rather feel peace, happiness and love? It really is entirely up to you. So choose love. It's much nicer. And you save thousands on therapy bills.

CHAPTER FORTY-SEVEN

The Circle

IT IS NOT HARD TO IMAGINE that there is a circle in your life. Those you love are inside the circle and those you do not love are outside the circle. This is not hard to imagine, is it? I think you can see this circle very clearly in your own life.

Inside this circle you have invited friends and family members. And maybe not even all your friends or family members. Some, like the aunt who is always criticizing you at family gatherings, you leave on the outside. Some who were once on the inside you may have moved to the outside because of something unforgivable they did to you. There are many more outside your circle than inside. And some of them switch positions.

For some, the circle becomes smaller as they grow older. Instead of growing to make room for the increasing numbers inside, the walls of the circle become more dense, like a fortress, and it becomes harder to welcome now ones in. And a number who were inside have been evicted. Fortunately this is not so common, at least for those on a spiritual path.

As our spiritual practice develops, our heart and our circle expand. We forgive what we have previously thought was unforgivable. We invite and welcome in those we evicted from the circle or never invited in. As the number of those inside our circle grows, somehow so do we. Our relationship with our family improves greatly as we invite more members into our circle of love. We begin to see that love is far more important than the petty grievances over past events that we once focused on so intently. We learn to forgive and move on. We find that we are healing, and that this healing is somehow affecting the entire family.

As we do this, we notice that our dear friends are not only increasing but our friendships are deepening. The number we welcome into our circle grows. And we do too.

At this point, the walls of our circle have become less dense. They are more transparent, more permeable. The separation between those inside our circle and those outside is becoming less obvious.

But still there are those outside our circle. There are those we do not invite in. At certain moments in our life, we meet people we tell ourselves we will never invite in. They are forever banned. The guy who cut you off on the highway, almost caused an accident and then had the nerve to give YOU the finger. He's definitely outside the circle. Way outside. And maybe there are others who you still cannot forgive, even though you are becoming aware that you should. What they did is still too painful and unforgivable. So they remain outside the circle. The neighbor who "accidentally" ran over your dog. You're sure it was more than an accident. He never liked your dog. You just can't bring yourself to invite him into the circle.

And there are many others you refuse to invite in. Do you really want to invite Hitler into your circle of love? Osama bin Laden? Or the politicians in that other party who are doing all those terrible things to your country?

Although your circle has been growing and you have too, there are still many outside the circle. There are many you don't want to invite in. And this is where the spiritual rubber meets the road.

Even inside our circle there are those we love more and those we love less. There are levels and gradations of our love. We love our children more than our neighbor's children. And we even have favorites among our own children. We love our present spouse more than our ex-spouse. And this even seems completely obvious that we should love in this way. Society tells us this is how we should love. We are doing it right, aren't we?

As we continue growing in love, we begin to understand that love does not have these rules, restrictions and limitations. These come only from our thoughts, beliefs and social conditioning. Our heart tells a very different story. Our heart only knows love itself. Our heart only recognizes love. It has no levels or gradations. It has no rules, restrictions or limitations. And we begin to notice something very interesting. It makes no choices about who is inside the circle and who is outside. In fact, to the heart, there is no inside and outside. There is no circle at all. There is only love.

We often call this unconditional love, and sometimes even Divine love, as if this were not something humans were capable of or at least a very lofty goal that only a few Saints ever attain. But this is just love. This is what love really is. And every human has experienced this, even though most are still unaware of it. This is the very nature of love itself. And even more than that, it is the very nature of what we are.

There is no circle. There is no inside or outside. There is no separation at all. This is what love knows. This is what love is. Your favorite child, your spouse, your best friend, your mother, your father, your Guru, God, Hitler, Osama bin Laden, the guy who cut you off on the highway, the neighbor who ran over your dog, all of these are only One. There is no separation. There is no higher or lower. There is no good or bad. There is only love. That is all there has ever been. This is what love means. This is what love is. This is what you are.

This is where the spiritual rubber meets the road. Some people are so easy and effortless to love. We invite them into the circle the moment we meet them. And this is wonderful. This is very, very good. But it is really those who are not so easy to love that have come to teach us how to love. This is where our spiritual growth is. These people are our teachers. They are our Gurus. The guy on the highway. The neighbor who ran over our dog. The aunt who always criticizes us. Hitler. Osama bin Laden. The politician who drives us crazy. These are our Gurus. They have come specifically to teach us how to love, how to really love.

As long as anyone is outside of our circle, our circle is not complete and we are not complete. We cannot know who we are as long as a single person out of 7 billion is still outside our circle. As long as a single human, insect, reptile, animal, blade of grass or a single stone is outside our circle, we cannot be complete. We cannot know who we truly are.

In Truth there is no circle. There never has been. There is no inside or outside. There is only One. There is only love loving itself in all these amazing appearances. But until you realize this for yourself, until you directly experience this, continue growing your circle. Continue forgiving and inviting and welcoming more into your circle. Continue bringing whoever is outside your circle into the love inside. Continue dissolving all disagreements and grudges, all fear and anger and grief, into love. The larger your circle, the closer you are to your True Self. Eventually the circle will dissolve all by itself, just as the dream of separation will.

This is a very good practice.

CHAPTER FORTY-EIGHT

You ARE Love

PLEASE DON'T IMAGINE that this is a philosophy, a theory, a spiritual teaching or anything that the mind can understand. It is simply the true essence of what you are. It is your True Self.

No one can ever take this away from you because it is what you are. No circumstance or situation can make this love any less than it is because it is what you are. You cannot be less than enough because love is never less than enough. It can only be exactly what it is. It can never be different from what it is. It cannot grow or shrink. It can never be absent. Only our conscious seeing of what we are can change.

When we are in love with another, we are only seeing ourself. We are experiencing this love that we are. We are seeing ourself in the other. Perhaps this is why when a relationship ends we feel we have lost something terribly valuable. We feel we have lost ourself or a huge and extremely important piece of ourself. We have become so used to seeing ourself projected outside that we have forgotten where the True Self really is. So when this mirror is no longer in front of us, it feels like we or a big part of ourselves are also no longer here. And that is very painful. Almost like an amputation of the heart. But really we have simply forgotten where to look.

All this time during the relationship it was simply showing us what we are. This love we felt is what we are. All the beautiful qualities in the other person were never other than our own

The Zen of Love

beautiful qualities. We were always looking in a mirror. And in a deep love, the mirror is very clear. It is showing us exactly what we are. So when the mirror is no longer in front of us, what we love the most seems to be gone.

But what the mirror was reflecting has not gone anywhere. It cannot go anywhere. The mirror can only reflect what we are. So this great love we felt is still exactly where it has always been. It is what we have always been. We simply need to turn around 180 degrees, and experience the very beingness of this great love that we are.

Every love affair is showing us this very thing. Up until now we have told ourselves that we needed a mirror to see this. We refused to see it as what we are. We had a very different idea that we were a separate, limited person who could only experience these things in certain situations. And we searched for those situations that would allow us to experience it. And that was a very good thing to do. A very good thing. Because each time we experienced this particular clear mirror, we came a little closer to seeing the source of that reflection. Who we really are. Our True Self. And of course, that felt wonderful.

What we truly are is the very source of love, peace and joy. And the absence of that mirror of course feels increasingly terrible. The contrast between the mirror and absence of the mirror becomes so painful that we are forced to look back to the source of the reflection. We have always known that this is freedom from the pain, from all pain, from all suffering. And when the pain becomes intense enough, we finally look. And then the miracle happens. We see that we are love itself, and have never been anything but love. And it is even more than the mirror reflected. Much more. More encompassing. It encompasses the entire universe. And simply doing this, simply realizing what we are, is the greatest gift we could ever give this world. And love cannot help giving. One man who did it had a religion created around him. It is really that powerful and profound.

CHAPTER FORTY-NINE

Unconditional Love

TO LOVE SOMEONE UNCONDITIONALLY with not even the idea of expectation is the greatest and most powerful magic the world has ever known – and yet nothing could be more ordinary, more simple or more obvious.

To love unconditionally has no conditions. You do not love because someone is beautiful, a wonderful lover, romantic, kind, loyal, does what you like, or for any reason whatsoever. You love for the sake of love alone. Love is its own condition. And love is the only condition. It does not matter whether the person you love loves you. That would just be another condition. Love is enough. You love simply because you love. There is no other reason. You could also call this falling in love with love. And since there are no conditions, it is the most natural and completely effortless form of love.

Few of us have been the beneficiaries of such love. It is very powerful. It may be the most powerful healing medicine that exists. It would be difficult for one who identified strongly as a separate person to love in this complete unconditional way. Persons have needs and expectations. And so they are often disappointed. Unconditional love can have no disappointment. There are no needs or expectations to disappoint. How can you disappoint love? And one who loves unconditionally is love itself. The idea of a separate person has dissolved, leaving only this great, unconditional love.

CHAPTER FIFTY

The Silent Saint

MY FRIEND SARAH NAEGLE lived as a Silent Saint. She lived an awakened life. But she never made a big deal about it. She simply lived a very normal life, with the one exception that she was free. Not all her life. None of us are. We need to experience the limitations of the dream first before we realize it was just a dream and return to the freedom that we are.

But Sarah, oh for someone so humble and unassuming, she attracted people to her like a magnet. Awakened people tend to do this. They tend to appear extremely attractive to those still living in the dream. They are like a bright flame or light is to moths. And this is because they are a bright light in this world. They glow from inside. And everyone can see this glow.

Although Sarah would never accept the title or role of teacher, she attracted a great many people to her. Just being in her presence was such a great teaching. People would come to her humble home in Sedona Shadows, just to be near her. And when she spoke, such wisdom would come from her mouth. But more than that, there was her presence, her glow, and her love – most of all her love. She loved everyone. And this was all she saw. All she saw in this world was love: in each person, in each thing, in each event. She lived a life of love and joy.

I learned so much from Sarah, and my gratitude is beyond what words can express. She taught me real love. She taught me what it is to be awake. Sarah had no ego, and no identification with her body. When she was dying, she used that to help us as well. It simply became another teaching, another way to use the body for communication of the only things that really matter: love, God, awakening. She told us that her body had been falling apart and was going to die soon. And she watched this happen in awe, wonder, love and joy, just as she watched all things. It did not bother her at all. She simply felt love and joy just as she did when her body was healthy. There was no difference to her at all.

Although many of us, myself included, felt quite sad to be soon missing this wonderful presence in our lives, she would remind us that this cannot happen. "The body is simply an illusion," she would say. "It's not really here. It just appears to be here. What is here is love. That's all." She would often say, "There is just love. That's all there is." It was so clear that she felt that and lived that. And this is why she helped so many people.

My friend Ahna called her the Silent Saint. And yes, that is a wonderful description. Of course Sarah would never accept a title like that. When people came to her for teaching, as so many did, she would simply say, "There are no teachers. We're just friends sharing Truth with each other." How beautiful. I miss you Sarah. Even though I know you are right here and could not be anywhere else. I love you. I am glad you were in my life, and I'm even more glad that you still are and helping me write this book.

Can I even imagine that Sarah is not helping me write this book right now? I know she is. She is writing this just as much as I am. Because in love, in Truth, there is really only one voice, only one set of fingers typing, only one heart. That's all. And that is the voice of love, the heart of love. That is the heart and voice of God. And this is what we have forgotten.

We see different bodies in this world. We divide things up into good and bad and make judgments about everything. But Sarah didn't do this. All she saw was love. And thanks to her, that is what I see now too. Thanks to Sarah I am awake. I'm sorry I'm crying a little. It's okay. It's a momentary thing. I can still get emotional. I would say that Sarah was more than my spiritual teacher. She was my spiritual mother. I've had so many, so many beautiful spiritual mothers and fathers. I am blessed beyond any concept of blessed. But I am also not fooled. I know that Sarah and all my other spiritual fathers and mothers, both living and long out of the body, are none other than love, none other than God, none other than me. And yet I feel enormous gratitude every moment of my life for their great contributions to me.

I hope you will read this book and feel Sarah too. I hope you will feel my friend Steve. I hope you will feel Mooji. I hope you will feel Thich Nhat Hanh. I hope you will feel Jesus and Buddha. I hope you will feel Ramana Maharshi and all the other great Saints and teachers who have gone before and will follow after. I hope you can feel them because they are here. Just as I am. Just as you are. We are never alone. We are never separate from everything that has ever existed. I'm sorry if I'm crying again. Please excuse me. There is great emotion in this, tears of gratitude, tears of love. Sometimes the gratitude and love are so powerful it would be overwhelming in a lesser body. And yet all these great beings are me and are also you. They cannot be anything else. We are simply talking to ourself in different appearances. We are simply guiding ourself back home.

I am awake. Yes, it is true. There are not that many of us in this world, although there are more than ever before in human history by my count. And this is wonderful. It is not a big deal. And yet it is the biggest deal there is for a human being. The entire cosmos sings when a single one of us remembers again who we truly are. It is enormous freedom, love and bliss. And somehow it is also a responsibility. Not in any burdensome way, but because we recognize that we are really all one. We owe to the other aspects or ourselves to help all of us come home. We are complete. We need not do anything ever again. This is very clear. And yet we do. Not from a sense of ambition. What would there be to be ambitious about? And who could accomplish anything? There is nobody to do this. We are pure Spirit, no longer a body or personality. It's not that we don't sometimes forget. That can happen for a while. I still do. Evidently that forgetting fades away completely eventually. And that will be nice. And I do feel that this forgetting is happening less and less, and it is rarer and rarer. I am very happy for that. But I am always happy. Only when I forget again for a moment can I experience anything less than happiness, love, peace and freedom. When I remember who I am, this does not happen. I am an awake being. My body still feels hungry when it is hungry. It still gets tired when I have not had enough sleep. It may even occasionally get a cold when it needs to detox itself. I now realize that colds too are only for my benefit and the body's benefit. Everything is. Everything is for my benefit, just as everything is for your benefit. Here is an interesting Zen story about this.

CHAPTER FIFTY-ONE

It Is All for Your Benefit

TWO ZEN MONKS were walking by a beautiful, tranquil pond. The sun was shining and glistening on the pond's surface. A gentle breeze created tiny ripples. A fat frog sitting on a rock was also enjoying the sun. Suddenly, shattering the tranquil silence, a huge white crane swooped down on the frog, and with great violence, tore it to pieces.

The younger monk, his peace of mind suddenly torn apart just like the frog, turned to his elder brother and asked, "Why does this have to happen?" This is a very human question, isn't it? How often have we asked similar questions when confronted with things we do not like or understand? Why are there wars? Why is there disease? Why is there poverty and oppression? Why is there death?

The elder monk replied with great wisdom, "It is all for your benefit."

It is all for your benefit. This may be hard to understand at first glance. How is war or disease or violence or death or poverty for my benefit? How are they for anyone's benefit? Yet everything that is created, everything that we create, everything we experience is for our own benefit.

This can be challenging to see if we have created cancer or some traumatic situation. For a long time we resist even being aware that we have created any of it. As this becomes clearer, we begin to look for the reasons why we created it. This often begins with a serious questioning about why a disease or traumatic situation appears. By serious questioning I mean that we throw out all the conditioned explanations, which are generally extremely shallow and usually far off base. We would not be living in a dream if these explanations were accurate.

We open our minds completely, and simply be with the question, until answers seem to arise by themselves. In this way we begin to realize the benefits of what previously seemed terrible, and we begin to realize the part we played in creating it. Eventually we begin to see that everything is for our benefit. Everything. It is a very great realization. If only it were as easy as a monk or friend telling you, "It's all for your benefit." But let this be a beginning. Let this be an opening. Let this begin the questioning.

CHAPTER FIFTY-TWO

I Am Only Writing to My Self

I AM ONLY WRITING to my Self and I am also reading as my Self. For there is nothing else that exists. As I look out upon a sea of faces, bodies, appearances of separation, I know that this is really not true. There is only one Spirit here. To my human eyes, to the body's eyes, it appears as many different people in many different bodies. How interesting. I used to believe this myself. Now I don't. It is what it is. There is only One Spirit here. And it can be felt, this One Self appearing as many. This is what it is like to remember. This is what it is like to remember who you are.

This is not a book so much as it is life. One life. Your life, my life, the 7 billion lives are all just this One Life. And this life is love because that is all there is. I know I keep saying this, but it is very important to realize this. There is only One. There is only Love. There is only God. And love is the pathway back to that. Love is the way back to God, to your True Self, which is really what this sea of faces and all these apparent bodies really are. People love me because I am love. There is an innocence about me, a beauty. People project many things onto it – sexy, handsome, kind, funny, compassionate and more – but really it is just love. That is all there is. That is what draws people like moths to a bright light. Remember when you were searching for a love mate and had trouble finding one. Suddenly you met someone and fell in love. When love blossomed in you, when you remembered for a brief time, just remember how all those men or women you were interested in now came out of the woodwork and were suddenly very interested in you. Before you felt this love, they barely noticed your existence. Now suddenly they are drawn to you as if you were a powerful magnet. This is the power of love. This is the power of you, of your True Self, which is not separate from love.

As love, you and I are not separate. We are not limited in any way. So I am writing to you with a deep, unconditional love, that perhaps you can feel. Perhaps you can feel this love coming through these words and even the spaces between these words. It is here. If you are aware, you can feel it. And in this feeling, you know that we are not separate. So I am writing to you and I am also writing to myself, for you see there is no difference. I am both teacher and student at the same time. I am both author and reader. There is no separation between the two. When we let love embrace us, the world of self and other dissolves. And what is left is only love.

CHAPTER FIFTY-THREE

I Love You

BY NOW YOU SHOULD KNOW what I mean when I say I love you, My Beloved. It means I see who you truly are. And maybe you now see this too. Maybe now you experience this One Heart. Maybe now you see your True Self. And this is not other than my True Self or the True Self of the infinite cosmos. This is how I can say that I love you. This is how I can say that I know you. This is how I can say that I see you. This is how I can say that I AM You. We are One, my Beloved. And this is always what love points to and has been pointing to all along. The only purpose of love is to clear away all imagined separation between us, to clear away all imagined separation between you and all that is.

Eckhart Tolle often says, "You do not have a life. You ARE life." Isn't that a beautiful way of saying it? You ARE life. There is no separation between you and anything that appears in your life. It is One Life flowing effortlessly. Knowing this, how can you resist it? How can you reject it? You are only rejecting yourself. How can you crave it, need it, or desire it? It is only you. You are already it. You are already totally complete and whole. You always have been. For just a moment, perhaps eighty or ninety years (not even a blink of time in eternity), you forgot, and imagined you were a limited, separate person. And now you are remembering, aren't you? Perhaps this book has helped you. Perhaps this book, along with other books,

The Zen of Love

teachers and life itself, have helped trigger this most ancient of memories, the memory of your True Self. The entire purpose of your birth has never been anything but this. And now it is happening. Hallelujah!

So, My Beloved, welcome Home. Perhaps you are now aware of the energy that runs through this book that you're holding in your hands. The love that awakens your True Self is in every word. But it is even more evident in the silent spaces between words. In the moment a passage resonates, and you take a breath and put the book down to allow your heart to absorb and answer this call, love is acting most strongly. Here's where it is doing its work. This book is not meant to be understood with the mind, but with the heart. It's not meant to be understood – it's meant to be experienced.

Now that you've experienced it, now that your Heart Song has been activated, your world and your life have changed. You may not notice this all at once. Some do. In others it takes some time. Whatever happens for you is exactly the perfect way for you. In love, as in life, there are no mistakes. Love and life are one and the same. And you are not separate from either. You may right now be feeling a calling to share your discovery with others. And this is as it should be.

Sharing this deep discovery is completely natural because there really are no others. Your mind may not yet understand this, but your heart has always known. We are One, you and I. And these seeming others are also this same One. And this is what love means. It is the falling away of the imagined separation we have, up to now, believed is life. It is a dissolving of what is not true. It is a dismantling of this dream of separation. This is falling in love with love. It is the Path of the Awakened Heart. And you are already on your way. Without your doing anything, including reading this book, it is already happening. It is working from within. It has been doing this since you took birth in this body. Your mind may still be telling you very different stories. That's fine. The mind is filled with conditioned

Discover Your Own Awakened Heart

thoughts and it takes time to shed them.

Your mind cannot understand what is happening. The inner work is happening anyway. Your heart already knows this. Your heart is where this work is happening. And it never fails. Success is guaranteed. It's not a matter of if, but simply when. And this when is perfect and inevitable. So don't worry. Relax. It's all happening exactly as it should. More and more you will notice love appearing in your life. At first you'll experience this as something happening outside you. You will be happy and grateful for it. But eventually you will notice where this experience of love is really coming from. And then your time in this dream of separation will come to an end. You will be free. You will be love. You always have been.

Much love to you, My Precious One. I am so grateful for our journey together.

Peter

When you live life as love
and see only love,
the world has no choice
but to reflect love back to you.
It is a perfect circle

Resources

You can find other teachings, books, videos, guided meditations, zen art, on-line workshops, Living Awake Groups, retreats, Satsangs and access to individual sessions with Peter on his website. Most of this is at no cost.

The Map of Consciousness – The Journey of Awakening is a step-by-step guide taking you through each of the seven stages of human consciousness from the first glimpse to full awakening. There are practices, meditations and resources specifically geared to each stage.

Not only are Peter's teachings available but you will find an extensive listing of resources of other awakened teachers. Each of us awakens in our own way and our own time. It's important to have as many resources as possible available so you find the right one for you. The goal, as always, is your awakening.

www.n-lightenment.com

About the Author

Spiritual teacher, healer, author and artist, Peter Cutler had a profound spiritual awakening at the tender age of twenty-two. Ten days after it began, he promptly fell back into the dream state most of us consider our lives. Not having a clue how this happened, he began a spiritual search that took him through many teachers, practices and traditions, finally flowering as this great light of profound peace, unconditional love and happiness.

The radiance of this awake being has a profound affect on people, often leading to remarkable healings.

For those who are ready, he assists in the birth of the awakened nature that lies within each of us. He offers weekly teachings, healing, Living Awake Groups, retreats and private sessions on-line or at his spiritual center in Sedona, Arizona (The Sedona Zendo of the Awakened Heart).

For more information about the author, teachings, videos, books, zen art, on-line workshops and meditation retreats, visit his website.

www.n-lightenment.com

Printed in Great Britain
by Amazon